ROCKY MOUNTAIN NATIONAL PARK
NATURAL HISTORY HANDBOOK

JOHN C. EMERICK

PUBLISHED BY
ROBERTS RINEHART PUBLISHERS
IN COOPERATION WITH
ROCKY MOUNTAIN NATURE ASSOCIATION

Copyright © 1995 Rocky Mountain Nature Association

Published in the United States of America
by Roberts Rinehart Publishers, Post Office Box 666
Niwot, Colorado 80544

International Standard Book Number 1-879373-80-7
Library of Congress Catalog Card Number 94-66091

Printed in Hong Kong
Cover photo by John Fielder
Back cover photos by Perry Conway
Book design by Ann E. Green
Illustrations by Susan Strawn and Bill Border
All maps © 1995 John C. Emerick

Distributed in the United States and Canada by
Publishers Group West

Publication of this book was made possible, in part, by a grant from The Greenwich Workshop, Inc., Trumbull, CT (with partial proceeds) from the sale of "Prayer for the Wild Things", an Art in Concert™ edition by artist Bev Doolittle and musician Paul Winter.

TABLE OF CONTENTS

WELCOME TO ROCKY

Rocky Mountain National Park straddles the Continental Divide and encompasses a region dominated by rugged peaks, evergreen forests, and alpine tundra—more than a quarter-million acres of the southern Rocky Mountains. Rocky Mountain is one of the highest parks in our National Park System. Here, elevations range from 7,600 feet near the town of Estes Park to 14,255 feet atop Longs Peak. More than 60 peaks in the park exceed 12,000 feet.

Ponds and lakes—nearly 150—nestle among park cliffs and forests. Scores of streams cascade down rocky slopes and through glacial valleys, eventually making their way to lowland deserts and prairies. The 50-mile drive from the east side of the park to the west offers an unusually diverse landscape: stately ponderosa pine, lush mountain meadows, primeval forests of spruce and fir, aspen groves, and moist valley bottoms filled with willow, river birch, and countless beaver ponds.

The park's real gem is the hundred square miles of bare rock and alpine tundra crowning the ridges and peaks above treeline. Here in

Andrews Glacier

Elk depend on meadows such as Moraine Park (right).

Golden eagle (below).

this open world above the forests, summer visitors can see herds of elk, bighorn sheep, mule deer, and a variety of smaller animals. Observation pullouts and trails leading from Trail Ridge Road, one of the highest paved highways in the United States, offer breathtaking panoramas of distant peaks and mountain ranges, as well as a dazzling array of alpine wildflowers.

Rocky Mountain National Park was established to preserve this natural environment and enable people to enjoy its wild treasures. Prehistoric peoples hunted in these mountains, trappers sought beaver in the valleys, and today about three million visit the park each year. Yet, most of the land has remained essentially the same as it was hundreds, even thousands, of years ago.

Recreation in the park is in keeping with its singular natural beauty. Visitor activities include hiking, fishing, camping, and climbing.

Sometimes travel and other activities are restricted to trails or specific areas in order to prevent the park from becoming over-used and damaged. In these and other ways, the National Park Service is managing the park to maintain its natural character for generations to come.

Because of its unique alpine environments, the park also is a site for scientific research. In 1977, the United Nation's "Man and the Biosphere" Program designated Rocky Mountain National Park an international biosphere reserve. The park contains prime examples of high-elevation ecosystems, so it is an ideal standard against which to measure the impacts of human activity on alpine environments. Researchers study mountain climate, air and water quality, ecology, wildlife management, and many other topics within the park. These studies contribute to an international program documenting global trends in the environment.

Above all, Rocky Mountain National Park is a place for people to enjoy and better understand nature. Take time to listen to the slap

Blueberry leaves in autumn

Mills Lake and Glacier Gorge in winter (above).

Great horned owls are year-round park residents (right).

of a beaver's tail in a willow-rimmed pond on a summer eve, the gravelly croak of a raven on a snowy winter day, the haunting whistle of a bugling bull elk in autumn, the lonely sound of a coyote howling at a Rocky Mountain moon. Delight in discovering a wood lily hiding among streamside alders. Watch millions of tiny diamonds of dew sparkle on a meadow at dawn or the primordial drama of a rabbit falling prey to a swooping golden eagle. This is Rocky! We invite you to experience its wildness, seek solitude in its hidden places, and perhaps learn something of nature's wisdom. Tread softly, and enjoy your stay.

Ponderosa pines in Wild Basin (right).

I

A BECKONING WILDERNESS

O verlooking park valleys and forests, Trail Ridge Road winds through alpine tundra 12,000 feet above sea level. No trees grow here, but during the summer the tundra blooms as a vast garden where myriad, colorful wildflowers dance in the mountain breezes. From here, you can gaze southward toward an imposing chain of peaks that bestrides the Continental Divide. Less than two miles away, their silent granite faces, weathered and broken over millennia, dominate the landscape.

They would be within a comfortable hiking range were it not for the deep, heavily forested canyon that lies between. This abyss is impassable to all but the most determined hiker, so most travelers are content to pause for a few silent moments to behold the awe-inspiring panorama. Tiny lakes shimmer in basins at the foot of towering cliffs and snowmelt waterfalls plunge down the sides of the canyon. In the early morning, when the air is still, you might hear the soft, bell-like notes of the horned lark, the trilling of a rock wren, or the muffled roar of the river as it tumbles down its boulder-strewn channel some 2,000 feet below.

Fifteen thousand years ago, perhaps when the first Stone Age human journeyed to this spot, this place looked much different. Then, ice filled the canyon and, during winter, snow covered all—except where wind scoured it from peaks and ridges. Summer warmth still fostered blooming wildflowers in these snow-free, rocky refuges, but the closest trees were many miles away and thousands of feet lower in elevation. A trek to this place would have been fraught with danger: icy crevasses, blinding storms, and starvation. The last great Pleistocene ice age still gripped the land and glaciers filled the high mountain canyons and valleys, covering nearly half of the 417-square-mile area that is now Rocky Mountain National Park.

Fresh snow on Hallett Peak (left).

The enormous erosive forces of the glaciers shaped the breathtaking vistas that capture the spirit and imagination of millions of people who visit this place. Jagged spires, sheer cliffs, and jewel-like alpine lakes are the legacy of these ancient rivers of ice. But the park's story does not end here.

ANCIENT HUNTERS

During the ice ages, tundra mead-ows carpeted virtually all of the park not covered by permanent snow and ice. The upper limit of trees was at about 8,000 feet, near today's east and west entrances. Precipitation was greater then, so forests extended eastward, far onto the plains. About 14,000 years ago, the climate warmed, dimin-ishing the heavy snows that fed the glaciers. Glacial ice began melting faster than it could be replenished by winter storms, and the glaciers started shrinking. It

Native American hunters.

took only a thousand years or so for the glaciers to recede into the heads of the valleys. By 7,500 years ago, they had disappeared. As the climate became warmer and drier, and the glaciers retreated, forests crept up the mountain slopes. By the time early American Indians hunted regularly in this region, treeline was probably higher than it is today.

The earliest people to visit the region remain a mystery. They left behind little to tell us about their lives, and we do not really know when they arrived. Archaeological evidence reveals that their ances-tors apparently migrated from Asia just before the end of the last ice age and may have been living on the high plains east of the Rockies as early as 13,000 to 16,000 years ago. Then, mammoths, woolly rhi-noceroses, giant bison, ground sloths, saber-toothed tigers, and other now-extinct mammals roamed the woodlands and prairies. We know that Stone Age people of the Folsom Culture lived in the foothills

11,000 years ago, and projectile points from earlier and later cultures have been found at sites along the Continental Divide in and near the park. These mammoth and bison hunters undoubtedly wandered across the mountains from time to time, but we have no evidence that they stayed.

Bison, mammoths, and other large animals meant food, clothing, sinew, and tools to these early peoples. These large mammals already were in decline, however, as the Pleistocene glaciers vanished. By about 7,000 years ago, many had become extinct, forcing hunters to rely more heavily on plants and small animals for survival. Thus, early peoples became better adapted for life in the mountains, and may have been drawn there to seek game during dry periods when food on the plains was scarce.

Remains of 4,000-year-old huts found near Granby, west of the park, suggest they may have lived in some mountain locations for extended periods and probably hunted regularly in the region. Perhaps these pre-historic peoples were the first to establish the Ute Trail, which winds across Trail Ridge and is named for a tribe that occupied the region thousands of years later.

Along Trail Ridge Road a row of stones, thickly encrusted with lichens, lies half-buried in the turf. The stones appear to be remnants of a low wall that has lain undisturbed for centuries. Further inspection of the site reveals a slight depression surrounded by a low screen of rock slabs—probably an ancient hunting pit. Perhaps this was the focal point of a game drive: a group of prehistoric hunters moving behind a herd of elk, bison, or bighorn sheep, trying to coax the nervous animals forward without causing them to panic and scatter. With luck, the low walls would turn the animals toward other hunters concealed in the pit or behind boulders and rock cairns. One mistake— a premature movement, or the clatter of a dislodged rock—and the herd would dash off, leaving the hunters empty-handed after hours of painstaking effort.

Dozens of such sites lie along the Continental Divide in and near the park, some constructed nearly 6,000 years ago. One, located near Mount Albion, south of the park, has 13 stone walls, 16 hunting pits, and 483 rock cairns. Because ancient hunting drives obviously involved considerable labor and large-scale cooperative planning, these structures likely were used again and again, perhaps for centuries.

Ute family.

About a thousand years ago, the Utes appeared in the region. Hunters and gatherers like the people that preceded them, they traveled throughout the region by foot. Then, in the late 1600s, a dramatic change occurred. The Utes began to acquire horses from Spanish traders. They became much more mobile and aggressive, often banding together with the Comanches to launch raids against the plains Apaches and Spanish settlers. On horseback, they also became more efficient bison hunters; hunting forays out of the mountains onto the eastern plains became commonplace.

The Rocky Mountain region was dominated by the Utes until the arrival of the Arapaho around 1790. The Arapaho were a relatively small group, but were skilled at riding horses, hunting bison, and fighting. Conflict between the Utes and Arapaho lasted for decades, until European-American settlers began to arrive in the mid-1800s. By the turn of the century, all of these American Indians had been relocated to government reservations, mostly outside Colorado. An important era in the human history of the region had come to an end.

It is difficult to measure the impact these early peoples had on their surroundings. The earliest hunted mammoths, giant bison, and other large, now-extinct mammals. Although early hunters may have depended on such animals, they also may have contributed to their demise; to what degree we will never know. Later hunting and gathering societies that regularly moved through the mountains undoubtedly had some effect on plant and animal populations; again, we can only speculate on their significance.

Settlers told tales—difficult to substantiate—of Indians setting forest fires to drive game or to confuse enemy tribes during raids. Although native people probably used other areas of the Rockies more heavily, we surmise that they were here and used this area's natural resources much as they did elsewhere. For the most part, it was not until European-American settlers arrived that significant and rapid changes to the regional ecology began.

Major Stephen H. Long.

MODERN DREAMS

Fur traders and trappers were probably the first European-Americans to visit the area of Rocky Mountain National Park. These dauntless people left no records, and their travels are poorly documented. Zebulon Pike and other noted explorers of the early 1800s never actually visited the park area, although an expedition headed by Major Stephen H. Long reached the base of the Rockies and traveled southward along the foothills. While in the vicinity, expedition members noted a high peak that towered above the surrounding range. That mountain would later be named after Major Long. Gradually, the fur trade increased, but it was the 1858 Colorado gold rush that drew large numbers of pioneers to the region.

Perhaps we can be thankful that miners never found much gold or silver here, because the land escaped the devastation that accompanied mineral development elsewhere in the Rockies. For a brief period during the early 1880s, a few hundred hopeful miners lived in Lulu City and Gaskill, small mining towns on the park's west side. Today, the decaying remains of a few log cabins are all that remain of those dreams of mineral wealth.

Like so many others, Joel Estes was first attracted by the gold rush, but saw other possibilities and became the first settler in a mountain valley later known as Estes Park. In the shadow of magnificent, snow-capped peaks and swooping valleys, Estes turned to ranching and hunting, selling the meat in Denver and other rapidly growing towns along the foothills. Others followed Estes, and homesteads appeared in valleys on both sides of the Divide.

If mineral wealth was not a lasting attraction, the scenery was. Enthusiastic writers such as Englishwoman Isabella Bird and William N. Byers, pioneering editor of Denver's *Rocky Mountain News*, extolled the area's virtues and helped attract a continuous stream of visitors that remains unabated to this day. Pioneers such as Abner Sprague found that tourist trade presented fewer hardships than cattle ranching and provided a more reliable source of income. Even the Earl of Dunraven, a wealthy Englishman who amassed an 8,000-acre cattle ranch in Estes Park during the 1870s, foresaw growing numbers of tourists and constructed a hotel. Resorts and guest ranches were built throughout the valleys and small rental cabins became commonplace. In 1909, F.O. Stanley, inventor of the Stanley Steamer automobile, completed his luxurious five-story hotel—The Stanley—that still overlooks the town of Estes Park.

The growing number of people increased demand on the region's natural resources. Nearby forests were cut for timber and firewood; willow and beaver were displaced by hay meadows in moist bottomlands; elk were extirpated; and water projects proliferated.

Visitors today wonder about a prominent scar high on the western side of Kawuneeche Valley, extending nearly the length of the Never Summer Mountains. It is especially obvious from Farview Curve along Trail Ridge Road. The scar marks the Grand Ditch, a 14.3-mile canal begun in 1890. The Grand Ditch intercepts water flowing from alpine basins high in the Never Summers, diverting it from the Colorado River watershed to the Cache la Poudre River east of the Continental Divide. Twenty feet wide and six feet deep at its widest point, the ditch was dug mostly by hand and took nearly five decades to complete.

The Grand Ditch is only one of many water diversion projects in the Rockies that carry water from the western slope of the Divide to the more arid eastern slope. Diversion projects such as these have been essential to the growth of towns and agriculture along the eastern foothills. At the same time, removing water from western slope streams fundamentally has affected natural flooding cycles, wetlands stability, and other ecological processes critical to many plants and animals.

The Grand Ditch was built in a time of accelerating change in the region. This and other mounting threats to the natural resources of the southern Rockies set the stage for the conservation movement that was to follow.

A NEW PARK IS BORN

By the turn of the century, increasing concern for land protection had prompted Congress to set aside a number of preserves. Yellowstone National Park was established in 1872 and others, including Yosemite, Sequoia, Mount Rainier, and Crater Lake, followed in the next two decades. In 1905, the area of today's Rocky Mountain National Park was included in the Medicine Bow Forest Reserve. Apparently, this was done without the approval of the region's leading citizens. Many living in the Estes Park area maintained that the forest reserve was designed to promote cattle grazing and timber harvesting and did not adequately protect natural resources.

Some of these residents, including Enos Mills, began a vigorous campaign to establish a national park. Mills, owner of the Longs Peak Inn and well known as a guide and naturalist, had perhaps the most extensive knowledge of the region. More important, he was an able speaker and a persuasive conservationist, and toured the nation enlisting support for his ideas. Finally, on January 18, 1915, after five years of debate

and compromise, Congress passed legislation creating Rocky Mountain National Park. On January 26, the bill was signed by President Woodrow Wilson.

Designation of the park signaled a new era of land management for the region, as well as increased pressure from visitors. Cattle grazing and hunting in the new park ended, and programs protecting wildlife and wildlife habitat were initiated. New trails and roads were built, including a road to Bear Lake and a second one over Trail Ridge.

Enos Mills (above); a park ranger during the 1940s (below).

Eventually, the National
Park Service acquired
much of the privately
owned property within park
boundaries and restored
this land to natural conditions. In the process, it
removed popular resorts
and lodges, such as Stead's

Ranch and the Brinwood Ranch-Hotel in Moraine Park, Fall River
Lodge in Horseshoe Park, Deer Ridge Chalet, and Phantom Valley
Ranch in Kawuneeche Valley. The Park Service built new campgrounds and established a quota system to limit backcountry use.
Many of these changes have been controversial, yet all were born of
a need to adhere to the Park Service mission: to provide a high-qual-
ity outdoor experience for visitors while protecting the park's natural
resources for future generations.

The Elkhorn Lodge was a favorite respite for visitors.

In the same vein, the Park Service feared that a proposed second major
water project would compromise the very wilderness values that the
park was formed to protect. They knew the environmental burdens
caused by the Grand Ditch, a water project built before the park was

Park visitors enjoy camping in the 1920s (above); campers today with a surprise visitor (right).

established and, thus, beyond much Park Service control. Despite Park Service objections, the demand for water was simply too great to be displaced by ideals of wilderness preservation. In 1937, President Franklin D. Roosevelt approved the Colorado–Big Thompson Project.

Today, Lake Granby, near the park's southwest corner, serves as the project's reservoir, collecting water from western slope streams, which then is pumped up to Shadow Mountain Lake. There, the water flows into Grand Lake and then through the 13-mile-long Alva B. Adams Tunnel. The water passes under the park to the tunnel's eastern portal, from there by siphon and two shorter tunnels to a power plant on the margin of Lake Estes, near the town of Estes Park.

In retrospect, the Colorado–Big Thompson Project appears to have caused little damage to the park. Because of environmental concerns voiced at the beginning of the project, the Bureau of Reclamation exercised great care during planning and construction phases to minimize effects on the natural setting.

Human occupation has left many marks on the landscape and ecology of the park. Ancient walls from prehistoric game drives have survived. The bison they hunted were eliminated long before European settlers arrived. Human use has subtly changed plant communities. Remnants of old roads and ditches offer clues to the locations of buildings, hay meadows, and stock pens of the pioneers. Lichen-covered stumps within the forest bear mute testimony to logging activities of past decades.

These marks, however, take away little from the majesty of Rocky Mountain National Park. It is a place where visitors can sense the powerful forces that thrust up, then sculpted the park's peaks and ridges. It is a place where miles of windswept alpine tundra overlook forests, streams, glacial lakes, and meadows, a place where visitors can see countless wildflowers and one of the largest concentrations of wildlife in the southern Rocky Mountains. Finally, it is a place that offers everyone recreation, solitude, and the grandeur of nature.

A park naturalist leads visitors on an interpretive hike.

Arrowleaf ragwort and chiming bells bloom next to Icy Brook in Loch Vale near Taylor Peak (right).

Cascade, along Glacier Creek Trail (below).

II

MAJESTIC MOUNTAINS
GEOGRAPHIC SETTING

With peaks soaring more than 6,000 feet over the plains and a ruggedness far exceeding that of mountains in eastern North America, Rocky Mountain National Park epitomizes the southern Rockies. Here, visitors are treated to expansive vistas and spectacular landforms. From vantage points on peaks and ridges, you can see northward some 60 miles to the Medicine Bow Mountains in Wyoming and south past the Indian Peaks and Mount Evans all the way to Pikes Peak, 100 miles distant. Fifty miles to the west, on the opposite side of a broad, intermountain valley known as Middle Park, lie the snow-capped peaks of the Gore Range. Beyond the Gores are the Flat Tops and the mesas and canyons of the Colorado Plateau. Scarcely 20 miles to the east is the rolling expanse of the Great Plains, extending like an ocean to the horizon.

The southern Rocky Mountains form part of the Continental Divide, the 10,000-mile-long spine of mountain ranges that stretch from Alaska to Patagonia at the tip of South America. The Divide is a major geographical feature that, like the crest of a roof, separates waters destined for the Atlantic Ocean from those flowing toward the Pacific. In North America, the Divide's highest elevations stand in the southern Rockies, which extend from southern Wyoming to northern New Mexico. In Colorado, 53 peaks rise 14,000 feet above sea level, and most of the southern Rockies is more than 8,000 feet high. Rocky Mountain National Park embraces part of the southern Rockies known as the Front Range, a 170-mile-long mountain range that rises abruptly from the Great Plains.

Contrasting with the park's mountains and ridges are its many picturesque valleys. The Alpine Tundra Museum on Trail Ridge Road commands a stunning overlook of the Fall River drainage, a steep valley that plunges between the shoulders of Mount Chapin and Sundance Mountain before meandering through the more level ground

The Sharkstooth, viewed from Andrews Glacier cirque (left).

of Horseshoe Park. Similarly, dozens of other valleys slice through mountain flanks, providing dramatic wilderness settings—some so remote that people rarely visit them.

In the Rocky Mountains, the term "park" often refers to large openings in the forest, especially valley bottoms. Thus, Moraine Park, Hallowell Park, Horseshoe Park, Paradise Park, and Summerland Park all refer to large mountain meadows within Rocky Mountain National Park. The national park is a public preserve; the "parks" within Rocky Mountain National Park are landscape features, not separate preserves. The town of Estes Park takes its name from the lush, grassy expanse that occupied the valley when the first European-American settlers arrived.

Perhaps the most inspiring places in the park—the quintessence of Rocky for many people—are the spectacular gorges that line the east side of the Continental Divide south of Trail Ridge. The names of natural features in these places flash vivid images of the land: Glacier Gorge, The Gash, The Sharkstooth, Chasm Lake, Chaos Creek, Emerald Lake, Solitude Lake, Sky Pond. Hiking into any of these gorges is like walking through an enormous cathedral with thousand-foot walls and rich, green tapestries. Many of the most popular hikes into these gorges begin at the upper end of Bear Lake Road, but visitors can find some of the best backcountry experiences in Wild Basin. Located in the park's southeastern corner, Wild Basin has scenery that is just as inspiring and attracts fewer people.

Poudre Lake, practically straddling the Continental Divide at Milner Pass, is the source of the Cache la Poudre River, named by French fur trappers who once cached gunpowder somewhere along its banks. The Cache la Poudre, like the Big Thompson and Fall rivers, flows eastward toward the Gulf of Mexico and the Atlantic Ocean.

Just a few hundred feet from Poudre Lake, on the other side of the Milner Pass parking area, is the Beaver Creek drainage. Water in Beaver Creek flows west into the Colorado River, whose headwaters are in the park's Kawuneeche Valley. In this peaceful setting, the Colorado is so narrow in places that you can jump from one bank to the other. A thousand river miles downstream from the park, the

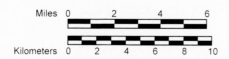

The weathered granite of Hagues Peak is reflected in the waters of Crystal Lake. These rounded forms are typical of the way many kinds of granite erode.

Colorado thunders through the colossal abyss of the Grand Canyon on its way to the Pacific Ocean. There, it is indisputably the major river of the southwestern United States.

Also on the west side of the park are the deep, glacial valleys of Tonahutu Creek, North Inlet, and East Inlet, and miles of scenic backcountry trails. All three of these streams flow into Grand Lake, just outside the park and the largest natural lake in Colorado.

THE RISE OF THE ROCKIES

The gray rocks of the park's mountains, twisted and fractured by herculean forces within the earth's crust, form a stark backdrop for the softer textures of forests and meadows. By human standards, the Rockies are ancient, their age measured by a time scale that defies the imagination. Geological evidence suggests, however, that the present mountains are young in terms of Earth's lifespan. In fact, these mountains were preceded by a succession of earlier ranges that alternately rose and wore away, each time followed by a different environment. Gazing upon the Rockies, we are hard-pressed to visualize the region covered by seas, sand dunes, swamps, and marshes. Yet, all existed here at one time or another.

Our record of these ancient environments lies in the sandstones, shales, and other exposed sedimentary formations that lie east and west of the park. For example, Red Rocks Park, west of Denver, and the Flatirons near Boulder are rock formations composed of sediments eroded from mountains that existed hundreds of millions of years before the present Rocky Mountains. Many such formations once covered the region, but they eroded as today's mountains rose from under the sediments of those ancestral ranges. Although only fragments of these formations remain within park boundaries, nearby discoveries of dinosaur bones, marine shells, and fern fossils testify to the remarkable changes in climate and landscape that have occurred here.

The present Rockies began to form about 70 million years ago with the first of several stages of crustal uplift. The most recent stage, five to seven million years ago, pushed the mountains to their present elevation.

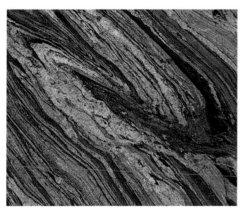

Banded gneiss.

Although the mountains are geologically young, most rock seen in the park is from 1,400 to 1,700 million years old. Much of the rock is metamorphic (gneisses and schists), formed of ancient sediments and volcanic deposits that were drawn many miles beneath the Earth's surface by massive crustal movements. Deep within the Earth's crust, these rocks were compressed, folded, and chemically altered by tremendous heat and pressure. In some places, this material was invaded by masses of molten rock. When it cooled and solidified, this molten material became granite. The granites, gneisses, and schists that were heaved thousands of feet above sea level form the core of today's Rockies. They make up Longs Peak, Stones Peak, Terra Tomah Mountain, Ypsilon Mountain, and most of the other well-known peaks in the central and northern part of the park.

New intrusions of molten rock and dramatic episodes of volcanoes and ash flows about 29 million years ago formed parts of the Never Summer Mountains and adjacent areas. Evidence suggests that Mount Richthofen, in the northern part of the range, is the remnant of an ancient volcano. Nearby Specimen Mountain is largely composed of lava and volcanic ash, although a steep depression known as "The Crater" probably was never a volcanic vent as its name implies. Lava Cliffs, above Trail Ridge Road south of the Alpine Tundra Museum, is also an accumulation of volcanic ash.

Distinctive black-and-gray stripes of banded gneiss, dark, fine-grained schist, and granite sparkling with its larger mineral crystals are all common in the park. Along Trail Ridge Road and in the backcountry, outcrops of these rocks are obvious and sometimes extensive. Gneiss and schist often weather into jagged peaks and ridges, such as Hayden Spire and The Sharkstooth. Granite frequently produces rounded forms, such as Lumpy Ridge, north of Estes Park.

NATURE'S FINAL TOUCHES

During the last few million years, tumbling streams have cut canyons and valleys; wind and moisture have slowly eaten away at the rocks. But of all the erosive processes that have shaped the Rockies during recent geologic time, the most significant is glaciation. During the ice ages, the mighty rivers of ice that occupied park valleys and much of the continent's northern latitudes were nature's supreme sculptors.

Geologic map of Rocky Mountain National Park (facing page), showing the widespread occurrence of granite (pinks) and metamorphic rocks (gray) throughout the park. Glaciation has left numerous deposits of till (greens) which forms moraines in most of the park's valleys. (Based on U.S. Geological Survey Miscellaneous Investigation Series Map I-1973, by W.A. Braddock and J.C. Cole.)

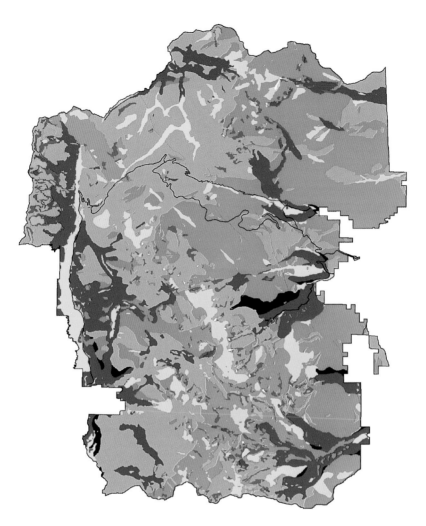

UNCONSOLIDATED SEDIMENTS

Alluvium in valleys (stream deposits)

Talus (rock fields on slopes and at cliff bases)

Rock glaciers (masses of rocks, presumably once with ice cores that permitted flow; some are still active)

Colluvium (other sediments on eroding slopes not included above)

Glacial Till

Holocene (less than 10,000 years old)

Pinedale (10,000 to 35,000 years old)

Bull Lake (130,000 to 150,000 years old)

BEDROCK UNITS

Sedimentary Rocks
Various formations, mainly Pierre Shale

Igneous Rocks
Volcanic rocks

Mostly granite less than 60 million years old

Mostly granite 1.3 billion years old or older

Gabbro of the iron dike

Metamorphic Rocks
Various types, mainly gneisses and schists

OTHER FEATURES:

Water

Permanent snow and ice

Major roads

Alpine glaciers appeared during periods when the climate became cooler and wetter than it is today. Summer's warmth was not great enough to melt winter snow and large snowfields began to accumulate. As snow gradually piled deeper, the bottom layers were compressed into ice. When the pressure of accumulated snow and ice became great enough, the ice began to flow downhill. With movement, the stationary ice fields became glaciers.

At times, snow deposition exceeded the amount of ice lost by melting and evaporation, so glaciers continued to grow. During extended periods of less precipitation or higher temperatures, however, the lower portions of glaciers melted at a faster rate than the downhill movement of ice, and the glaciers shrank.

The erosive action of the glaciers comes largely from their ability to quarry underlying rock. Water seeps into fractures in rock, freezes and expands, then thaws. The freeze-thaw cycle loosens fragments of rock, which then can be plucked, or quarried, by the glacial ice and carried away. Rocks thus entrained in ice can then act as grinding stones. As glacial ice flows downward, these rocks further grind out the sides of valleys. During the ice ages, glacial action over thousands of years widened valleys and steepened their sides, resulting in the characteristic U-shaped cross sections of the park's major valleys.

Such quarrying and abrasion also produced singular landforms. Quarrying plucked out rocks at the high, narrow tops of valleys, creating steep-walled basins called cirques. These glacial headwalls may lie next to one another; in some places, adjacent cirques are separated by narrow saddles, or cols, and jagged knife-edge ridges called arêtes. Pagoda Mountain, adjacent to Longs Peak, is a good example of a horn—a pyramid-shaped peak formed by several intersecting cirques. Prominent knobs of rock hard enough to resist glacial erosion are seen in Moraine Park and upper Glacier Basin. Such rocks are called *roches moutonnées* (French for "sheep rocks") because they often look like the rounded backs of sheep.

Interestingly, most of the park's cirque basins occur along east-facing ridges, but rarely on west-facing sides. For example, Trail Ridge,

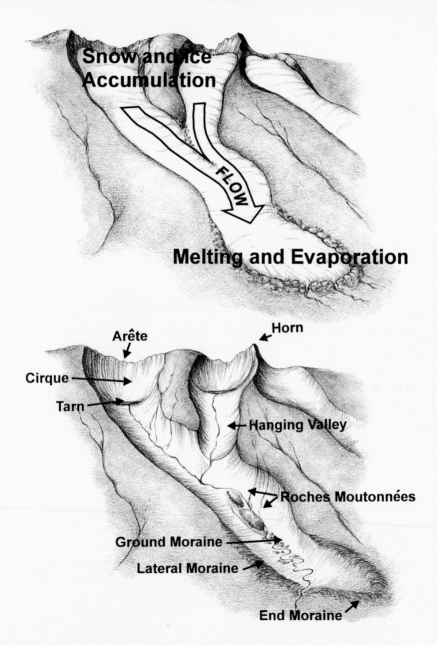

Snow and ice
Accumulation

FLOW

Melting and Evaporation

Arête

Horn

Cirque

Tarn

Hanging Valley

Roches Moutonnées

Ground Moraine

Lateral Moraine

End Moraine

Glaciers filled many of the park's valleys during the ice ages (above), and produced various landforms that characterize the high elevation terrain of today's Rocky Mountains (below).

Moraine Park, Glacier Basin, and Wild Basin offer vistas of dramatically carved eastern faces. The west-facing backsides of these rugged peaks are, for the most part, gently rounded. Prevailing winds caused this pattern. During the ice ages, winds blew mostly from the west—as they do now—and the mountains acted like enormous snow fences, allowing howling winter winds to remove snow that had fallen on the western slopes and deposit it in gigantic snowfields on the mountains' eastern sides. These snowfields spawned the glaciers that sculpted the numerous east-facing cirques.

Many glacial landforms in the park result from deposits of till—rock fragments of all sizes quarried by the glaciers and carried in the glacial ice. As the ice melted, this till was deposited at the margins of the glaciers and eventually formed ridges, called moraines. Moraines formed along the sides of a glacier are lateral moraines; those formed at the extremity, or snout, of a glacier are end, or terminal, moraines. Melting glaciers also left carpets of till on valley floors, often called ground moraine. These different types of moraines can be seen throughout the park.

Researchers, studying moraines found in the southern Rockies, have concluded that several periods of glacial activity occurred here. The oldest moraines found near Rocky Mountain National Park date from 300,000 to 750,000 years ago. These highly weathered tills are located in the St. Vrain valley near the town of Allenspark and in the vicinity of Lake Granby. If earlier glaciers were present, their deposits apparently were scoured away by younger glaciers or other erosional processes, or have become so weathered they are difficult to recognize.

More recent glaciations include the Bull Lake glaciation, two major advances that occurred 130,000 to 150,000 years ago, and the Pinedale glaciation, which began about 35,000 years ago and ended about 12,000 years ago. During these glaciations, ice filled all of the park's major valleys—as much as 2,000 feet deep. End moraines from these two periods lie near east entrances to the park and near the southern end of Shadow Mountain Lake west of the park. The longest glacier in this area was the 20-mile-long Colorado River Glacier in Kawuneeche Valley. Situated within a horseshoe bend of the

Continental Divide, this glacier was fed by numerous cirques and ice fields from both sides of the valley.

The largest, most prevalent moraines within the park are from the Pinedale glaciation. Some of the biggest Pinedale lateral moraines— located on the north and south sides of Moraine Park, Horseshoe Park, and Glacier Basin—are 800 feet higher than adjacent valley bottoms.

Bull Lake moraines are less common, but because Bull Lake glaciers were larger, remnants of their moraines are often found beyond the

The map at the right shows the approximate coverage of the park by ice during the maximum extent of glaciation. The positions of today's major roads are shown for reference.

The Gorge Lakes (below) are nestled in a glacial cirque. They are actually tarns, which are lakes that occupy depressions scooped out of the bedrock by the glacier.

*I*ce-age glaciers did not etch every park ridge and peak. Many peaks rose above the great glaciers and ice fields. This unglaciated land has also been molded by cycles of freezing and thawing—in this case, by frost action. Although frost action affects glaciated terrain as well, its effects are most obvious in the high country. Over thousands of years, the wedging action that occurs each time water expands as it freezes in soils and rock fractures has produced periglacial features unique to high mountain environments. Such features include block fields, or felsenmeer (German for "sea of rocks"), along broad saddles and ridges; slopes of stone rubble (called talus); and various types of patterned ground.

Patterned ground, found above treeline, often occurs as rock polygons and stone stripes (inset, above). Rock polygons usually occur on flatter ground and consist of stones that form rough geometric shapes enclosing turf centers. Stone stripes—parallel rows of stones separated by bands of turf—occur on steeper slopes and are elongated versions of rock polygons. Such phenomena apparently are the result of a process called frost heaving which separates larger rocks from the soil. Triggered by wetter climates of the past, most patterned ground in the southern Rockies is inactive today. A good place to see patterned ground, as well as felsenmeer, is from the Tundra Nature Trail on Trail Ridge.

reaches of Pinedale till. Bierstadt Lake, above Glacier Basin, fills a depression in a large body of Bull Lake till.

The last 12,000 years have seen intermittent periods of glacial advance and retreat, but glaciers rarely have extended far beyond their cirque basins. During periods of extreme drought and warmth, the glaciers disappeared completely. Today, ice movement occurs in a few snowfields, such as found in Andrews and Tyndall cirques. Although, technically, these snowfields are glaciers, they are barely surviving today's climate.

Although ice-age glaciers have disappeared, other processes continue to erode the mountains. This erosion is imperceptible to us unless a catastrophic event, such as a landslide or flood, suddenly moves a large amount of earth. Each year, loose soils and other material creep down the steep sides of valleys, aided by water, burrowing animals, and the footsteps of humans, deer, elk, and other large mammals. Occasionally, good-sized portions of earth will slump toward the valley floor, uprooting a few trees in the process.

Some of this material falls into streams that carry it farther down-valley, depositing it in flood plains. The flat, lower ends of Kawuneeche Valley, Moraine Park, and Horseshoe Park are actually the tops of thick sediment deposits carried downstream. This sediment buildup has also filled ponds and lakes left by the glaciers.

From mountain uplift to erosion by wind, water, and ice, the landscape of Rocky Mountain National Park has been molded by a number of processes. Although these processes occur over thousands, even millions of years, they are ongoing. The mountains continue to change; streams continue to carve deeper into the earth. In future millennia, other environments will exist here. Perhaps the Rockies will erode and new mountains take their place. Climates, too, change. At some point, large-scale glaciation likely will return to the region. Knowing that change—no matter how slow or how minute—has occurred, is occurring, and will occur allows us to appreciate the dynamic nature of the park's landscape and the fact that we are experiencing only a brief moment of geologic time.

III

MOUNTAIN CLIMATE

Most of the three million people who visit Rocky Mountain National Park each year travel in the relative comfort of their automobiles. With heaters and air conditioners, visitors can insulate themselves from the extremes of mountain climate. Many summer days, the weather is downright pleasant, even hot; at other times, it can be extremely cold, windy, or wet. Park weather is typical of continental climates far from the moderating influence of oceans or other large bodies of water. Conditions can change rapidly and unpredictably from warm and sunny to cold and stormy, and back, in less than an hour. In July, for example, visitors may become sunburned in the intense morning light, then encounter a snowstorm at higher elevations later that day. If you are contemplating an outdoor excursion in the park, you must be prepared for all types of weather, regardless of season.

As you travel to the park from lower elevations, there is a distinct change of climate. Temperatures are cooler; precipitation is more likely; winds are stronger; and, because mountain air is thin, the sun's intensity is greater. In general, summers are pleasant, with lots of morning sunshine, but winters are cold and windy.

Mountainous terrain causes the local climate to vary considerably from one place to another, depending on elevation, the direction a site faces, and whether a site lies on ridgetop, slope, or valley bottom. The description of park climate given here is brief and general, not only because of such variables, but also because only a few weather stations exist in the area.

A general rule of thumb is that air temperature decreases about 3.5 degrees Fahrenheit with each thousand feet of elevation gain. Therefore, higher elevations usually have cooler average temperatures than lower elevations, although this pattern is disrupted by cold air drainage in valleys. Average annual temperatures above treeline are

Glacier Creek in winter

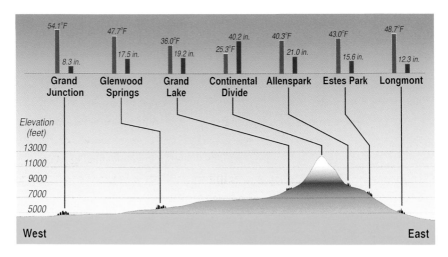

A climate transect crossing the Southern Rockies from east to west in the vicinity of Rocky Mountain National Park shows that higher elevations are generally colder and wetter than lower elevations. Average annual values of temperature (red bars) and total precipitation (blue bars) are shown for selected sites; based on data from the Colorado Climate Center in Fort Collins and the University of Colorado Institute of Arctic and Alpine Research.

below freezing, whereas the average annual temperature at Longmont, 20 miles east of the park at the base of the foothills, is 49 degrees.

Because cold air is heavier than warm, it sinks into valley bottoms from adjacent slopes. As a result, average temperatures in such valleys are often lower than on surrounding higher areas; subfreezing temperatures occur even during summer. In mountain climates, gardeners and farmers are especially concerned with the length of the growing season (the average number of days between the last "spring" frost and the first frost of "fall"). In Colorado, locations lower than 6,000 feet generally have growing seasons of 150 days or more, whereas elevations above 8,000 feet usually have growing seasons of 40 to 60 days. Places subjected to cold air draining from valleys experience even shorter growing seasons.

Near the park's west entrance and at the intersection of North Inlet, East Inlet, and Kawuneeche valleys, the town of Grand Lake counts a growing season averaging only six days. Grand Lake residents can expect freezing temperatures at any time of the year, but a visit to

Grand Lake will reveal that many plants grow there, and do well. Most are native species adapted to frequent summer frosts and thus have an effective growing season of three or four months.

Because the Rockies form an enormous barrier to air masses crossing the continent, they profoundly affect precipitation patterns. Moving air masses are forced to rise as they encounter the mountains. Because air chills as it rises, water vapor in the air condenses, forming rain or snow that falls to earth. Precipitation resulting from air masses rising over mountains is called orographic precipitation (from the Greek word *oros*, meaning mountain). Eastbound Pacific air masses are an important source of moisture to the region, particularly during winter months.

In spring and fall, moist air from the Gulf of Mexico frequently enters eastern Colorado and is pushed against the eastern slope of the Front Range, resulting in so-called upslope storms. During upslope storms, rain or snow falls on the east side of the park while the west side usually remains dry and, often, sunny and pleasant.

Mule deer buck

Late spring usually signals the onset of the thunderstorm season, which lasts through the summer. Thunderstorms, or convective storms, result when air warmed by the earth's surface rises rapidly. The air cools as it rises; because cool air holds less water than warm, moisture begins to condense. Convective storms tend to develop earlier in the day over mountain areas than over surrounding lowlands because, at higher elevations, solar radiation is more intense and heats air more rapidly. Storms begin forming over the mountains in late morning and intensify during the day as they receive additional heat from land surfaces. Usually, the storms drift eastward with the prevailing winds, often forming violent hailstorms and tornadoes on the plains. Summer weather in the Rockies typically consists of sunny mornings, stormy afternoons, and clear nights.

Although mountain storms may drift eastward, precipitation in the park is greater than on the plains. The reason is that average annual precipitation usually increases with altitude. The plains east of the Front Range are relatively arid, receiving about 15 inches or less pre-

A snow plow opening Trail Ridge Road in early June of 1983. Under normal conditions, the Park Service opens the road by Memorial Day, but this is not always possible.

A December scene (above) from Emerald Lake trail, looking southeast toward Longs Peak.

Inset shows a ranger collecting snow depth and water content measurements used to predict spring runoff.

cipitation a year. In contrast, high ridges along the Continental Divide in the park may receive as much as 40 inches annually. (Although this figure includes the amount of water contained in snow, actual snow depths often are much greater.) At higher elevations and on the western slope of the Front Range, precipitation tends to be uniform through the year. On the eastern slope, most precipitation occurs during spring and summer as a result of upslope and thunderstorm activity.

Much of the park's annual precipitation falls as snow. Snow cover during winter and spring is never uniform, however, because it is redistributed by wind. Prevailing western winds usually blow snow from the west-facing slopes of high ridges, whereas deep snow usually accumulates on east-facing slopes. Wind also blows much of the snow that falls on the mountain tops into forests just below treeline. Because of this effect, upper coniferous forests receive the greatest precipitation—snow accumulates five feet deep or more in some areas.

Even at lower elevations, snow cover is highly variable, depending on wind exposure and the amount of evaporation and melting that takes place on a given site between storms. For example, snow depth is regularly recorded at Hidden Valley and Bear Lake, both on the east side of the park at approximately the same elevation. Average annual snow depths on April 1 are 18 inches at Bear Lake and 11 inches at Hidden Valley. Deer Ridge, near Hidden Valley and only 500 feet lower, averages five inches of snow on the same date.

Throughout the park, subtle differences among plant communities are directly related to the distribution of snow. The snow depth in a particular location influences the amount of residual soil moisture available to plants through the growing season. At high sites covered by deep drifts,

Wind-sculpted spruce banner trees.

many plants do not begin growing until the drifts have melted. Snow cover also provides an insulating blanket that prevents underlying soils from deep freezing, protecting plants and animals that otherwise would be unable to survive.

Wind is a prominent feature of mountain climates. Typically, average wind speeds are greater at higher elevations. Above timberline, it is almost always windy. The wind blows most fiercely on peaks and

Sunrise on the Continental Divide with Taylor Peak in the clouds.

ridgetops. During winter, winds that scour these high places frequently gust at hurricane force. Although prevailing winds are from the west, peaks and ridges alter wind direction by channeling winds along canyons and valleys. During upslope storms, winds blow from the north-east or southeast.

A phenomenon known as the valley wind also may change the direction of air currents. On sunny afternoons, air heated by warm mountain slopes rises and moves up-valley as a gentle breeze. At night, lower surface temperatures cool the surrounding air, which becomes heavier and begins to sink. This colder, heavier air results in a breeze blowing down-valley in the early morning hours.

Solar radiation, another aspect of mountain climate, is more intense at higher elevations because the atmosphere is thinner. Thin air cannot filter out ultraviolet wavelengths as effectively as denser air at lower elevations, so sunburns occur rapidly. Air also tends to warm and cool more quickly because of its lower density. South-facing slopes receive more solar radiation than north-facing slopes and thus are warmer and drier. One result: distinctly different plant communities often occur on north and south sides of valleys.

At higher elevations, the effects of intense solar radiation are offset by increased cloud cover. More than 80 percent of summer days have at least partially cloudy skies, usually resulting from convective storms during the afternoons. Orographic activity during winter months often produces cloudy conditions over the high country for days at a time.

All of these climatic variables fundamentally affect plant development, including the onset of growth in spring, the timing of flowering and seed production, even the shape of plants, such as tundra plants that hug the ground to avoid the wind. For animals, climate influences seasonal behavior patterns such as hibernation, migration, and reproduction. Some species, such as the long-tailed weasel, snowshoe hare, and white-tailed ptarmigan, change their colors coincident with changes in season. Climate is largely responsible for the distribution of the major ecosystems found in the park—from warm, dry montane forests to windswept alpine tundra.

Moraine Park, looking west to the Continental Divide.

A break in the clouds following an afternoon thunderstorm, looking toward the Mummy Range from Trail Ridge Road.

One of the most serious dangers to hikers and climbers at high elevations is the lightning that accompanies summer thunderstorms. In the early stage of a storm cell, the developing thundercloud appears white with a flat bottom (A, opposite page). As the cell continues to develop, moisture continues to condense and turn the cloud gray—and hikers should take notice (B). The danger sign is the appearance of virga—wisps of precipitation that begin to stream from the base of the cloud, obscuring its flat bottom (C). Lightning strikes between clouds and the ground usually commence with the virga stage. Because these storm clouds can move rapidly and with little warning, hikers should leave exposed ridges and tundra slopes before virga is evident. Hikers should start hikes into the high country early in the day in order to be on the way down from exposed elevations by the time the thunderstorms arrive.

Besides the threat of lightning, thunderstorms may present other dangers. In late July 1976, one unusually violent thunderstorm stalled a few miles east of Estes Park, dropping 10 inches of rain and hail in just a few hours. The resulting flood tore through Big Thompson Canyon, killing at least 139 people.

A

B

C

IV

FROM FORESTS TO TUNDRA
PATTERNS ON THE LANDSCAPE

Traveling from the lowest elevations to the top of Trail Ridge Road, park visitors experience a change of climate roughly equivalent to a trip from Denver to the Arctic Circle. Such an abrupt climatic change produces a remarkable array of plant communities over a short distance—only eight miles, as the raven flies, from the park's main entrances to the Continental Divide. Ecosystems progress from warm montane forests interspersed with meadows and shrublands, through cool subalpine forests, up to alpine tundra.

At any location, plant communities are often deceptively diverse. Visitors might encounter spruce-fir forests mixed with stands of lodgepole pine and aspen groves, or with meadows. Meadows might be dominated by grasses, yet some parts might be covered by a profusion of wildflowers while other sections might be claimed by shrubs. Even the plant community beneath the shrubs may reveal a mosaic of different mosses.

Patterns of plant distribution are controlled not only by changes in elevation, but also by factors such as the availability of moisture during the growing season and the amount of snow accumulation during winter. Plant communities of warm, south-facing slopes can differ markedly from cooler north-facing slopes that lie just across a valley. Soil types also affect plant distribution. Soils that have developed on glacial till, for example, often harbor different species than soils formed from decomposed granite.

Disturbance by wildlife, humans, fire, avalanche, landslide, or other causes adds another important variable. Disturbed plant communities progress through a series of often long-lived transient phases—a process called ecological succession—until a relatively stable climax community is achieved. Aspen groves and lodgepole pine stands, which are plant communities that usually occur early in ecological succession, are common landscape features.

Hiking near Mchenrys Peak

Despite such diversity, most of the park's ecosystems can be grouped into a few easily recognized major types. These include riparian and aquatic ecosystems, mountain meadows and shrublands, montane forests, sub-alpine forests, and alpine tundra. Riparian ecosystems occupy moist soils alongside streams and lakes at all elevations. Mountain meadows and shrublands occur in a variety of sites, ranging from moist to relatively dry or rocky. Montane forests are warmer, drier forests at elevations generally below 9,000 feet while subalpine forests occupy the cooler, wetter, higher elevations up to treeline. The largest unforested ecosystem in the park is alpine tundra, which crowns all the mountain slopes above treeline.

Elephantella, usually found in wet areas at higher elevations, is a species that also occurs in the Arctic.

A moist spruce-fir ecosystem along Lion Creek in Wild Basin.

Each of these ecosystems is described in the following sections. This book is intended to be a companion to the many excellent field identification guides that are listed in the back, by describing ecological relationships that control the distributions of some of those organisms found in the guides. Only common names of plants and animals are used in the text; however, equivalent scientific names are given in the index.

The distribution of the major ecosystems of Rocky Mountain National Park is shown on the facing page. The same map has been superposed on a three-dimensional shaded relief image of the park region above, which depicts a bird's-eye view looking toward the northwest. Alpine tundra, shown in pale yellow, dominates higher mountain slopes and ridges. Forests of ponderosa pine, shown in orange, are found only at lower elevations on the park's east side where the climate is warmest and driest. Large expanses of medium green, representing lodgepole pine forests, are shown on both sides of the park. The prominence of lodgepole pine results from numerous forest fires in the past, and attests to the importance of fire as an important ecological factor that has influenced the park's landscape patterns.

Both figures were developed from the park's geographical information system, a computerized data base created by the National Park Service for management of biological and other resources.

	TUNDRA		SPRUCE/FIR		LIMBER PINE
	ASPEN		DOUGLAS FIR		LODGEPOLE PINE
	MEADOWS		RIPARIAN		PONDEROSA PINE
	WATER		ROCK		MAJOR ROADS

N

Riparian Lands and
Aquatic Environments

S treams and lakes are like magnets, drawing people to their banks
and shores. A trail that follows a tumbling stream delights the ear
as well as the eye. And what avid hiker hasn't made a lake the goal of a
day's outing? Although the park is known for its rugged peaks, expansive forests, and spectacular vistas, its watery environments deserve
attention, for they are vital to the park's ecology.

Lakes, streams, and the riparian communities that border them occur
throughout the park and support the greatest plant and animal diversity in the park. They provide wildlife with water, food, cover, and places
to breed. Migrating birds frequent these places during spring and fall.
So, too, do bird watchers and other nature enthusiasts.

Riparian Ecosystems

The vegetation that grows along stream banks and shorelines is different from that on surrounding uplands. Plants that require or tolerate
plentiful water thrive here, often forming dense communities.
Riparian ecosystems include many kinds of plants. Water-loving
species intermix with those of the surrounding forests and meadows,
providing a variety of animal habitats.

Snowmelt, rainwater, and groundwater discharged by surrounding
slopes feed streams and wetlands at alpine and subalpine elevations.
Willow and dwarf birch shrubs intermingled with wet sedge meadows
fill the highest of these stream valleys. Because the wetlands in these
upper drainages often make soggy footing for hikers, most trails bypass
these places. A few amphibians are well-suited to this environment,
however, and such sites are likely places to encounter western toads,
striped chorus frogs, perhaps even a rare wood frog.

Below 9,000 feet or so, riparian vegetation becomes more diverse.
Willows are joined by river birch and thin-leaved alder. Aspen are
common, and blue spruce appear in the valleys. Narrow-leaved cotton-

Pond lilies on Cub Lake (left).

wood are numerous at some lower elevations, and a close relative, the balsam poplar, grows in scattered locations in Horseshoe Park, Moraine Park, and Wild Basin.

Riparian zones change more than any other type of ecosystem. Streams are restless, constantly eroding their banks or depositing new sediments. In flat valleys, streams tend to meander, widening their bends and occasionally short-circuiting them, leaving the abandoned meanders to form oxbow ponds. Floods that result from snowy winters and wet springs may scour channels or form new stream courses. Streambank vegetation is always at risk of being uprooted. On the other hand, stream deposits provide fresh surfaces for plants to colonize, oxbow ponds eventually fill with sediment and vegetation, and the cycle starts anew.

American dippers (left) are seldom far from streams. Adults submerge themselves completely as they glean aquatic insects from rocks below the surface.

Recently introduced near the park, moose are frequently seen on the park's west side (below).

Beavers profoundly influence riparian ecosystems. The dam-building ability of these large rodents is legendary; in many areas, beaver activity determines vegetation patterns as much as do stream dynamics. A pair of beavers can convert a section of riparian forest into a pond almost overnight. The subsequently waterlogged soils kill plants whose roots cannot tolerate an oxygen-poor environment and favor rushes, sedges, and other species that thrive in such soils.

The beaver's favorite food is the inner bark of aspen, willow, alder, and river birch. What beavers do not eat of these woody plants, they may use for construction materials. After they build an initial dam and lodge, they continue to excavate canals and build additional dams out of twigs, logs, mud, and sod. All of this activity is aimed at establishing a system of waterways that the beavers use to float materials they have cut, while minimizing the distance they must travel over land where they are most vulnerable to predators. Their main pond also serves as a winter larder. Beavers harvest twigs and branches that they anchor to the bottom and use as food after the pond's surface has frozen.

Eventually, beavers deplete the supply of materials in one area, forcing them to move to other areas. As their dams fall into disrepair, the ponds drain or become filled with sediment; then sedges and grasses take root. With time, willows and alders return to the area. On lower slopes, aspen, once cut by beavers, sprout again from their roots. In a decade or so, when the vegetation has recovered, beavers usually return to begin the process again.

Valley bottoms altered by beavers and shifting stream channels often display a striking patchwork of different plant communities. Dying oxbow ponds nestle among stands of willow, birch, and alder, which in turn fit like puzzle pieces between lush meadows of Canadian reedgrass and sedges. Here and there, beaver activity floods new ground, occasionally killing conifers that have encroached too far onto the valley floor. Old hay meadows created by ranching before the park was established have disrupted this natural mosaic in some valleys, but natural patterns are slowly re-emerging.

Such a rich diversity of habitats fosters an equally rich diversity of animals. Lincoln's, song, and white-crowned sparrows call loudly from streamside shrubs and western jumping mice, deer mice, and voles scurry through the thick grasses. These small rodents are stalked by coyotes and red foxes, who stop and listen for a moment, then pounce on their prey. Visitors commonly spot muskrats, which look like pint-sized beavers, as they paddle in ponds, lakes, or quieter stretches of streams. Mink swim and hunt along some park streams; and river otters, restored to the park's west side in the late 1970s, ply streams in that area of the park. The silvery bodies of water shrews are sometimes seen darting about streams in search of insects to satisfy their voracious appetites.

In the late 1970s, the Colorado Division of Wildlife also introduced moose to Colorado north of the park, near Walden. Several migrated into Kawuneeche Valley, and have become permanent residents. Moose sightings are now common in the valley and, occasionally, they are seen wandering east of the Divide.

Moose are the largest members of the deer family, with the biggest bulls approaching 1,200 pounds. They prefer wetlands, where they feed on aquatic vegetation during the summer and depend on willows and other shrubs in winter. Though moose tend to be more solitary than elk, they occasionally mix with elk herds. Unpredictable animals, especially during the October mating season or when females are nursing their calves, moose are best observed from a distance.

AQUATIC ECOSYSTEMS

The park is filled with watery environments, from ephemeral ponds lost in the forests, to glacial lakes and shimmering tarns set high in cliff-bound cirques. Multitudes of tiny rivulets merge into streams, which meet to form rivers. Life exists in these places, too, though not as conspicuously as on land. Trout that swim in the park's streams and lakes represent only a small segment of the aquatic fauna and thrive largely because of the healthy food chains that support them.

To a large extent, aquatic life in the mountains depends on the amount of nutrients in the water. The waters of the highest lakes and streams are cold and appear nearly as pure as distilled water. (They often contain microscopic parasites such as Giardia, however, which can cause severe distress to humans.) These waters have had little opportunity to dissolve minerals from soil and rocks, and thus contain few of the nutrients necessary for aquatic plant growth.

Streams at high elevations have steep, boulder-strewn channels where water tumbles in noisy cascades. Although this continuous agitation produces water rich in dissolved oxygen, the scarcity of mineral nutrients produces little aquatic plant life. The main energy source for microorganisms and invertebrates (mostly aquatic insects) that form the base of the food chain consists of leaves and other plant fragments that fall or wash in from adjacent forests and meadows.

The mineral content of aquatic environments increases at lower elevations mainly because mineral-laden groundwater percolates into the streams and lakes and organic nutrients filter in from surrounding land. Nutrient accumulation fosters the growth of a slippery film—periphyton—that covers submerged rocks. Periphyton consists of blue-green bacteria, various algae, and water moss. Although its slick surface can prove hazardous to hikers attempting to cross a creek, it is a critical food source for insects and other invertebrates. Because of periphyton, there are more aquatic animals at lower elevations than at higher ones. Although currents are usually too swift to allow the growth of larger aquatic plants, some plants do grow in the quieter pools of streams.

Many species of aquatic insects live in streams, mostly as larvae. Where the current is swift, the streamlined bodies of these larvae reduce their risk of being swept away. Claws, hooks, friction pads, or suckers enable many of them to cling tenaciously to submerged rocks and branches. Some, such as blackfly and caddisfly larvae, depend on sticky secretions to anchor themselves to objects. Others simply avoid the current, living instead under or between rocks. As protection against predators, caddisfly larvae often live in portable cases to which they attach grains of sand or gravel, which serve as ballast and camouflage.

Feeding habits of aquatic insects vary. Some scrape rock surfaces to feed on periphyton. Others gather fine organic fragments by crawling along the bottom or by filtering the water. Still others feed on leaf fragments and the stems of aquatic plants. In addition, some prey on insects or other animals, including fish larvae. Stoneflies, mayflies, caddisflies, and true flies (especially blackflies and midges) comprise the majority of insects in the region's streams. Of these, stoneflies are the most common in colder waters.

Aquatic insects, in turn, serve as an important food for most fish, including trout. Trout feed mainly in shallow "riffles" where the current is swift and periphyton-covered rocks support large numbers of insects, then return to quieter pools to rest.

Native cutthroat trout were once abundant in mountain streams of the southern Rockies. More than a century ago, however, non-native trout, including brown, rainbow, and brook trout, were introduced to area streams. As a result of the competition, cutthroat populations declined and are now limited to the highest, steepest streams. Although the Park Service stopped stocking non-native species in the late 1960s, their populations still persist at lower elevations.

For several years, the Park Service has maintained a program in Hidden Valley and other areas to enhance native cutthroat popula-

Greenback cutthroat trout

tions. As a result, greenback cutthroat can usually be spotted from the boardwalk that crosses Hidden Valley beaver ponds. Fathead minnows, white and longnose suckers, and johnny darters are some of the other fish found in park streams.

The numerous lakes that dot the landscape of Rocky Mountain National Park come in many shapes and sizes. And their origins vary. Some, such as Gorge Lakes (seen from Trail Ridge looking across Forest Canyon), fill depressions where bedrock was scoured out by glacial quarrying. Others, such as Forest Lake and Bierstadt Lake, formed behind dams of glacial moraine.

Some lakes are much newer. One formed in the upper end of Horseshoe Park on the morning of July 15, 1982, when the irrigation dam at Lawn Lake broke, sending a catastrophic flood down Roaring River. The flood carried piles of rocky debris to the valley floor, damming Fall River. Like a large beaver pond, this shallow lake will gradually fill with sediment and give way to marsh and meadow.

Fall River (below) gently meanders through Horseshoe Park.

A mile down-valley lie Sheep Lakes, which some geologists think are kettle ponds, created thousands of years ago when half-buried blocks of glacial ice melted. A number of small pothole ponds formed by weathering of exposed bedrock lie among the granite outcrops along Lumpy Ridge. The largest of these is Gem Lake, a rain-fed pond without inlet or outlet.

Not only is each lake unique, each lake's ecosystem is unique, depending on specific elevations, water chemistry, annual temperature variations, shorelines, and bottom characteristics. Because current greatly influences ecology, life in these still waters often differs markedly from that in streams. Larger aquatic plants are common. Just as important are microscopic plants, called phytoplankton, that drift in the open water and are a vital food source for other tiny organisms.

Cobalt-blue lakes of the high cirques may look inviting to anglers, but unless they are deep, they usually lack fish. High, shallow lakes—ice-covered in winter—do not hold enough oxygen for fish to survive. If fish are present, cold temperatures slow their growth and reproduction, and similarly inhibit the organisms they eat. In general, low amounts of nutrients make alpine lakes relatively unproductive.

Lakes at lower elevations support larger, more diverse communities. Aquatic vegetation growing in the shallows provides shelter and nourishment for insects and other invertebrates, and serves as a nursery for trout fingerlings.

Ponds and lakes are among the most temporary features of the landscape. Though they may seem long-lived in terms of human generations, lakes gradually fill with sediment and become shallower and smaller. Because they trap nutrients and organic materials, lakes and ponds also become more productive as they age. Nymph and Cub lakes, for instance, are rich in organic sediments; thus, they are filled with lily pads and other aquatic plants.

Freshwater sponges encrust submerged logs and myriad tiny organisms swarm the water. Copepods, scuds, and water fleas feed on millions of microscopic algae. They, in turn, are eaten by diving beetles, minnows, and other small predators. Leeches and flatworms that crawl among the

Tiger salamanders are common near ponds and lakes (above).

Chiming bells (inset top) grow along all of the park's water bodies; mountain wood lilies (inset left) are much rarer.

plants often fall prey to dragonfly nymphs or predacious beetle larvae. Northern leopard frogs, striped chorus frogs, and tiger salamanders live here, as do a variety of ducks and shore birds.

The park is dotted with so many small ponds that most are not found on maps. Among the most intriguing are the ephemeral ponds, which are often filled with thousands of delicate fairy shrimp, all swimming on their backs. When these ponds dry up, usually by late summer, where do these creatures go? And where do they come from next summer? The answer lies in their eggs, which survive in pond sediments, waiting until the next year when melting snows again fill these small depressions.

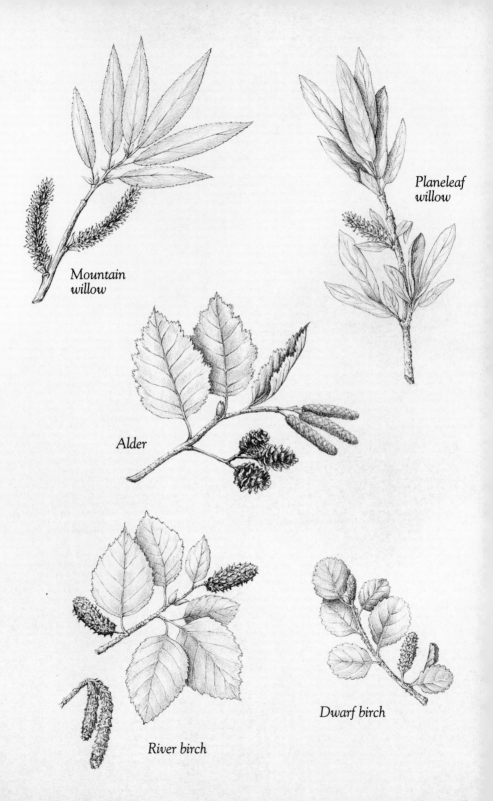

Mountain
willow

Planeleaf
willow

Alder

River birch

Dwarf birch

Riparian Ecosystems at a Glance

R iparian ecosystems are found along streams and rivers, as well as around the margins of ponds and lakes. Most riparian ecosystems in the park are dominated by shrubs: dwarf birch and various willow species at higher elevations, and at lower elevations, alder, river birch, and aspen join the willows. A few narrowleaf cottonwoods and blue spruce appear near park boundaries, but these trees are more numerous downstream of the park.

LOOK FOR THESE SHRUBS NEAR LAKES & STREAMS:

Mountain willow *The most common large willow, growing to nearly 18 ft. tall, found in the park's lower stream valleys up to 9,000 ft. elevation.*

Planeleaf willow *One of the most common high-elevation willows, grows to about four feet tall, and often forms dense thickets alongside subalpine streams.*

Alder *A large shrub found up to 10,000 ft., the alder may grow to a height of 15 ft. or more. The woody female catkins persist on the branches for up to a year. They look like miniature pine cones and are a good feature to help recognize this shrub.*

River birch *Another large shrub similar in appearance and distribution to alder. Younger branches have smooth red bark with white horizontal markings (called lenticels) that help distinguish this shrub from alder.*

Dwarf birch *Usually growing to a height of four to six feet, this small shrub is most common in boggy places and streamsides above 9,000 ft.*

PLANTS AND ANIMALS TO LOOK FOR:

Other Shrubs:
Chokecherry
Common gooseberry
Mountain maple
Red-osier dogwood
Shrubby cinquefoil

Mammals:
Beaver
Montane shrew
Montane vole
Muskrat
Raccoon
River otter
Water shrew
Western jumping mouse

Wildflowers & Other Plants:
Arrowleaf ragwort
Aquatic sedge
Bittercress
Canadian reedgrass
Chiming bells
Cow parsnip
Field horsetail
Giant angelica
Mountain woodlily
White bog orchid

Butterflies:
Atlantis fritillary
Ruddy copper
Titania's fritillary
Weidemeyer's admiral

Reptiles & Amphibians:
Northern leopard frog
Tiger salamander
Western terrestrial
  garter snake
Western toad

Birds:
American dipper
Common snipe
Green-winged teal
Lincoln's sparrow
Mallard
Song sparrow
Spotted sandpiper
Wilson's warbler

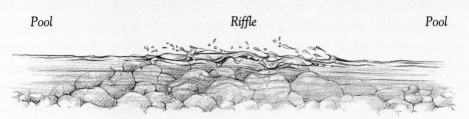

Pool   *Riffle*   *Pool*

The slower water in pools provides a resting place for fish. The rocky bottom in shallower riffle zones harbors greater numbers of aquatic insects. Riffle zones are important feeding areas for fish.

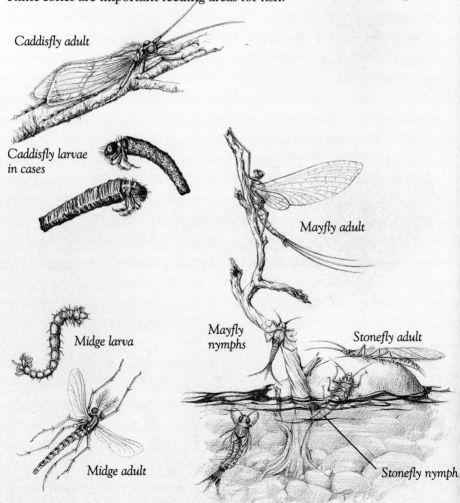

Caddisfly adult

Caddisfly larvae in cases

Mayfly adult

Midge larva

Mayfly nymphs

Stonefly adult

Midge adult

Stonefly nymph

Life in Ponds and Along Lakeshores

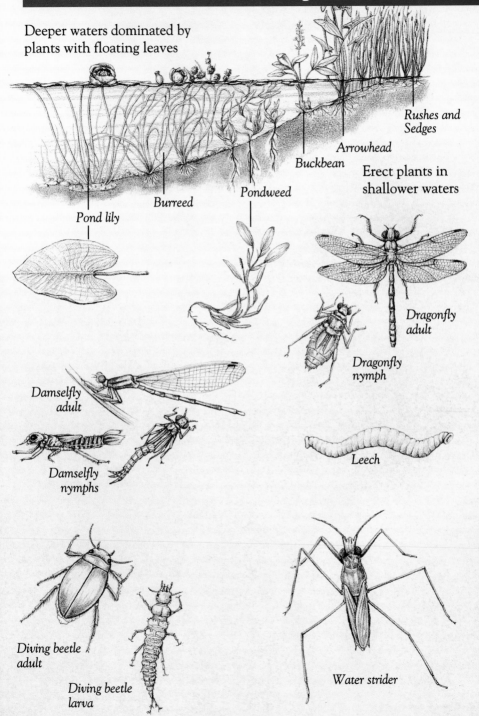

Deeper waters dominated by plants with floating leaves

Rushes and Sedges

Arrowhead

Buckbean

Erect plants in shallower waters

Burreed

Pondweed

Pond lily

Dragonfly adult

Dragonfly nymph

Damselfly adult

Damselfly nymphs

Leech

Diving beetle adult

Diving beetle larva

Water strider

MOUNTAIN MEADOWS
AND SHRUBLANDS

L ate spring is one of the best times to visit the park's lower meadows. Lengthening days and warmer temperatures bring sky-blue patches of Rocky Mountain iris and yellow fields of golden banner. Green-tailed towhees loudly proclaim their nesting territories from atop shrubs along the forest edge, and families of chipmunks and ground squirrels busily rummage for food among the grasses. Come evening, the patient observer, sitting quietly and inconspicuously, might be rewarded by seeing an elk tentatively enter the meadow. Soon it is followed by another, then another, until 20, 30, or more elk spread out across the meadow, feeding on tender spring shoots.

More than mere openings in the forest, these meadows and shrublands produce a rich mix of herbaceous vegetation that is key to the survival of the park's large elk herds. Many other animals also depend on open areas, such as Harbison Meadow on the park's west side and Beaver Meadows on the east. Wyoming ground squirrels, which resemble miniature prairie dogs, live exclusively in the park's meadows, as do vesper and savannah sparrows. Mountain bluebirds often nest in aspen along the forest edge, feeding in meadows and frequently imitating flycatchers by capturing insects in midair.

The grasses, wildflowers, and other low herbaceous vegetation that characterize meadows make these areas among the most colorful places in the park. Most of these plants require open, sunny conditions. Bright yellow western wallflowers, showy purple and pink splashes of penstemon and locoweed, and the large red-and-yellow heads of gaillardia adorn drier montane sites. Moist subalpine meadows blaze with fluorescent pink and red paintbrushes, blue chiming bells, and yellow arrowleaf ragwort as well as other sunflower-like blossoms.

Shrubs are usually present in meadows and sometimes become the dominant form of vegetation. Such shrublands can occur at various elevations and in a variety of conditions. Montane shrublands in Harbison Meadow

Golden banner in Moraine Park; Rocky Mountain iris (inset).

and on the south-facing slopes of Beaver Meadows and Hallowell Park are composed mainly of mountain sagebrush and antelope bitterbrush, which tolerate relatively dry soils. Shrubby cinquefoil, familiar in gardens throughout the Rocky Mountain region, often abounds in places with moderately moist soil. Willow or dwarf birch usually dominates wet sites, forming dense patches in subalpine and lower alpine areas.

The origin of meadows and shrublands differs from one place to another. Often, such habitats mark places either too dry or too wet for forest growth. Under these conditions, meadows and shrublands may be relatively long-lived landscape features. For example, broad subalpine and montane valley bottoms tend to accumulate fine-grained soils that, when kept moist by a high water table, rarely support tree growth. Mounds of well-drained glacial till and landslide debris within such valleys are exceptions, and on these drier "islands" trees may grow.

Another exception lies in the center of Moraine Park. There, soils have accumulated atop a large knob of bedrock called a *roche moutonnée* (see page 28). Ponderosa pine grow on these drier soils, creating a small island of forest surrounded by meadow.

The upper Cache la Poudre River valley, seen from Trail Ridge Road, provides another example of tree growth limited by soil conditions. Spruce and fir thickly cover the sides of this symmetrical, U-shaped glacial valley. The forests stop in an abrupt, regular line, however, near the valley floor, which is filled with meadow vegetation and willows. People wonder if the edge of the forest, so straight along both sides of the valley bottom, is artificial. It is not. Soil saturated during much of the growing season by groundwater percolating down from the valley's sloping sides inhibits tree growth on the bottom.

Forest fires, avalanches, high winds, and other disturbances also cause forest openings. Except for active avalanche paths, these areas may return to forest in a decade or two if undisturbed and if soil and climatic conditions are favorable. Near treeline or in dry montane sites where herbaceous vegetation has become well established, forest regeneration may take considerably longer.

A view of Longs Peak
(above) from Moraine
Park.

Mountain bluebirds(right)
nest in aspen cavities, but
feed in meadows.

Wyoming ground squirrels
(below) are abundant
in the park's meadow
environments.

*T*he beginning of autumn is marked not only by the golden hues of aspen, but also by a noticeable restlessness among the park's elk herds. There is not a more majestic animal in the park than a full-grown bull wapiti—the Shawnee Indian name, which means "white deer" for the animals' light-colored spring coats. The largest bull may weigh 1,000 pounds or more, with graceful, curving antlers that spread nearly six feet.

In September, the bulls' snorts and whistles begin to echo through the forests, and aggressive encounters become more frequent. By early October, mating season is in full swing and the bugling of the males is punctuated by the sound of crashing antlers as dominant bulls spar for the right to mate with a harem of cows. This annual drama attracts thousands of visitors who line the roads along the park's lower meadows for a glimpse of this wapiti mating ritual.

Like other members of the deer family, bulls shed their antlers each year, usually by late winter. Growth of a new rack begins a few weeks later and is completed by September. With so many elk in the park, one might expect to see the ground littered with fallen antlers. These bony leftovers, however, are a welcome source of minerals for rodents, who gnaw at them until scarcely a trace is left.

Elk are gregarious grazers. In the early morning and evening, herds of various sizes enter meadows to feed on grasses and other herbaceous vegetation—the bulk of their diet. In late spring, pregnant cows break away from the herds to bear their calves, usually born in June. Because of their size, elk have few predators. Coyotes and bobcats may take young calves temporarily left unattended by their mothers, but mountain lions are probably the park's only remaining predator capable of killing a mature elk, particularly if it is old or sick. Once, though, gray wolves and grizzly bears also preyed upon elk in this area.

In recent years, National Park Service biologists have become concerned about damage caused by large elk herds. Their browsing has killed numerous aspen; in some areas, elk have decimated willow and sagebrush shrublands. Fewer aspen means fewer places for cavity-nesting birds to live. In the tundra, severely browsed shrubs result in declining ptarmigan populations, which depend on willow buds for food during winter and early spring.

View of the Mummy Range from Horseshoe Park, with shrubby cinquefoil in the foreground (above).

Crab spider (right) waits on blossoms for unwary pollinators.

Above, one of the more commonly seen predators, a coyote, peers from its den.

A dietary mainstay of the coyote is the cottontail rabbit (left).

Some alterations are brought about by humans. In the past, for instance, the Park Service and other government agencies aggressively suppressed every forest fire. Over the years, forest growth eliminated much of the meadowland upon which elk depend. Few new meadows were being created by fire and, as a result, available winter range decreased. With a greater understanding of fire's role in an ecosystem, the Park Service now lets some fires burn if weather conditions are appropriate and human life and property are not at risk.

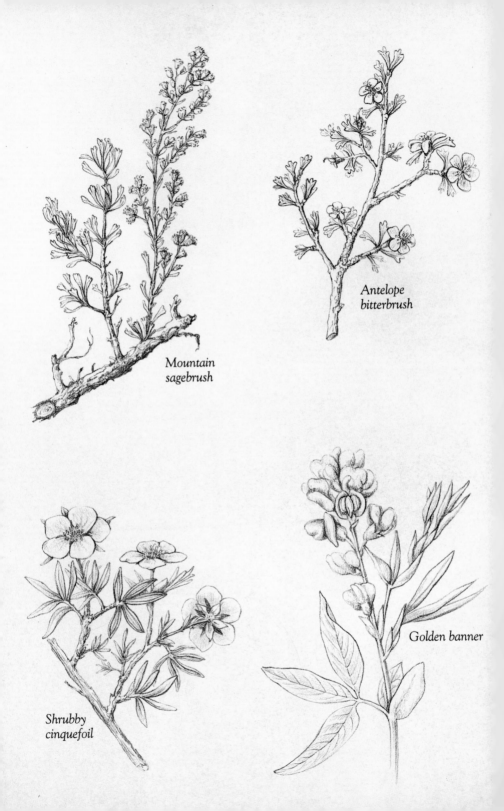

Mountain
sagebrush

Antelope
bitterbrush

Shrubby
cinquefoil

Golden banner

Meadows and Shrublands at a Glance

Meadows and shrublands are often downward extensions of tundra meadows near treeline or are moist places associated with riparian ecosystems. However, many meadows and shrubby sites are found throughout the park wherever soil conditions are unfavorable to tree growth, or where disturbance has created forest openings. Such places are especially common at lower elevations near all of the park entrances, where you will find many of the plants shown here.

Mountain sagebrush
Look for this gray-green shrub on drier places in Beaver and Harbison meadows. It has triangular leaves with usually three teeth at their tips.

Antelope bitterbrush
Often found with big sagebrush, this shrub has a similar leaf shape, but is a darker green. In spring or early summer, it is covered with small cream-colored blossoms.

Shrubby cinquefoil
This small shrub grows in moister places than sagebrush, but prefers drier soils than do the riparian willows. Its summertime profusion of nickel-sized yellow blossoms make this plant a favorite of urban landscapers.

Golden banner
This pea, with its bright yellow springtime flowers, grows in large patches in many of the park's lower meadows.

PLANTS AND ANIMALS TO LOOK FOR:

Other Shrubs:
Dwarf rabbitbush
Serviceberry
Various willows
Wax currant

Mammals:
Badger
Colorado chipmunk
Elk
Golden-mantled
    ground squirrel
Montane shrew
Montane vole
Northern pocket gopher
Wyoming ground squirrel
Yellow-bellied marmot

Wildflowers & Other Plants:
Black-eyed susan
Blue-eyed grass
Bluegrass species
Colorado locoweed
Dandelion
Fringed sage
Gaillardia
Grama grass
June-grass
Mountain muhly
Needle-and-thread
Sego lily
Sulphur flower
Tufted hairgrass
Wild strawberry

Birds:
American kestrel
Common nighthawk
Lincoln's sparrow
Mountain bluebird
Savannah sparrow
Vesper sparrow

Butterflies:
Common blue
Common sulphur
Painted lady
Phoebus parnassian
Red admiral
Ridings satyre
Ruddy copper
Weidemeyer's admiral
Western tiger swallowtail
Western white

MONTANE FORESTS
PONDEROSA PARKLANDS

A massive tree stands on a slope overlooking Moraine Park. Its lower branches are as large as the trunks of many lesser members of its species, and it would take several people holding hands with their arms outstretched to encircle its girth. For centuries, this forest patriarch has survived attacks by fire, insects, and weather. It was already a tree of considerable size when the first European-American trappers visited the region in the early 1800s. It witnessed the homesteading of the valley by Abner Sprague in 1875, the construction of other ranches, lodges, and cabins in subsequent decades, and the removal of most of those structures by the National Park Service in the 1950s and '60s. Over the centuries, it has provided shade to countless deer and elk, hunting perches for untold numbers of eagles, hawks, and owls, and nesting places for a host of smaller birds. Many nearby trees, some now quite large, have grown from its seeds.

This old tree—flat-topped, scarred, and ponderous—epitomizes the ponderosa pine. One of the most widespread conifers in the western United States, it is the largest species of conifer in the park. Here, 400-year-old giants grow taller than 150 feet and have trunk diameters of three feet or more. A mature ponderosa has a distinctive appearance: a broad, open crown, usually with a rounded top and a large, straight trunk with thick, reddish bark. Their olive-green needles, growing in bundles of two or three, are unique among Rocky Mountain conifers because of their great length, ranging from five to seven inches.

Ponderosa grow in a variety of situations and commonly are found mixed with other conifer species. They extend from the foothills of the Rockies (about 5,600 feet) to nearly 10,000 feet. On shady, north-facing slopes at low to middle elevations, ponderosa usually mix with Douglas fir. Above 9,000 feet or so, they are accompanied by Engelmann spruce, subalpine fir, Douglas fir, and often limber and lodgepole pine.

Ponderosa pines, Horseshoe Park. A great horned owl (inset).

Ponderosa are best adapted to drier, sunny, south-facing slopes at lower elevations. Here, they attain their largest size in an uncrowded forest or parkland. Strolling through ponderosa stands on a warm summer afternoon, park visitors may detect a piney, resinous aroma suffusing the air and the sweet butterscotch scent emanating from ponderosa bark.

Because ponderosa are usually widely spaced or grow in small groups, grasses, shrubs, and wildflowers cover the ground around them. This profusion of understory plants and an abundance of animals helps make ponderosa forests the most diverse of the park's conifer ecosystems. Almost any time of day, mule deer browse among ponderosa or lie in their shade. The robin-like song of the solitary vireo and the raucous calls of Steller's jays are common, as are the sounds of mountain chickadees, pine siskins, dark-eyed juncos, nuthatches, and mountain bluebirds. If you are lucky, you may spot the tassel-eared Abert's squirrel, unusual among park mammals because it lives exclusively in ponderosa forests.

Abert's squirrel (right); bighorn sheep (below).

Steller's jays are common throughout the park's conifer forests. A pasque flower blooms in early spring (inset).

Any plant that endures the hot summer harshness of such dry sites must possess some mechanism to withstand drought. In the case of the ponderosa, its long taproot penetrates below the sun-baked topsoil to draw moisture from deeper layers of soil. This tap root also gives the tree great stability, allowing it to withstand gale-force winds. A toppled ponderosa—its roots pulled from the ground—is an exceptional discovery. More often, wind-thrown individuals have fallen because the trunk has snapped, usually after the wood has been weakened by carpenter ants, beetles, or decay.

Ponderosa woodlands support a relatively large number of shrubs and herbaceous plants, so late summer ground fires are a frequent threat. Fire plays an important role in the ecology of the ponderosa by eliminating smaller trees and maintaining the sparseness of the woodland. The tall trunks and thick bark of large trees help ensure their survival during grass fires. Only when ponderosa become crowded do devastating crown fires threaten the mature trees.

Normally, the dense understory inhibits germination of ponderosa seeds, but when fire, animal grazing, or other disturbances reduce the ground vegetation, sun-loving ponderosa seedlings appear. If not killed by fire, the young trees will soon compete with older ones for moisture and nutrients. Eventually, this competition leads to stress, poor health, and susceptibility to insect attack and other forest diseases.

Such conditions lead to periodic outbreaks of the mountain pine beetle, a bark-boring insect that ravages ponderosa forests from time to time throughout the Rocky Mountains. When epidemics occur, trees often die in large numbers. Many ponderosa killed during a major epidemic in the late 1970s remain standing on the park's east side. Like fires, epidemics serve to thin the forest, but sometimes it is sad to see a tree that has survived centuries of hardship succumb to the brief toil of insects.

Large ears and antlers are typical of mule deer, the park's most common deer species. The broadtailed humming-bird (right) breeds in montane forests.

Mountain lion populations have increased in many Southern Rocky Mountain areas. Lions are occasionally seen in the park.

While nature's measures may seem severe, nothing is wasted. Old snags and fallen trunks provide nesting sites and food supplies for a variety of birds and mammals. A host of wood-boring beetles, ants, spiders, mites, and other invertebrates quickly invade the dead wood, speeding its decay. Even in death, the trees are part of the food chain, sustaining life, and slowly returning decades of accumulated energy and mineral nutrients to the forest.

The ponderosa that greet visitors entering Rocky Mountain National Park from the east are among the region's best examples of ponderosa parklands. Large stands of these stately trees in Horseshoe Park, along Deer Ridge, and in Beaver Meadows and Moraine Park serve as reminders of what many areas in the Rockies looked like before lumbering. Here, ponderosa forests reach an ecological climax. Barring major disturbance or significant climatic change, these forests will remain essentially unchanged. Big and resilient, set against a backdrop of rugged peaks, ponderosa help define the character of the eastern side of the park.

Ponderosa Pine

Ponderosa Parklands at a Glance

*T*hese open forests dominated by ponderosa pine are found on sunny, dry, south-facing sites from lower elevations up to 9500 ft.. Look for them near the Fall River and Beaver Meadows entrances to the park, and in Horseshoe and Moraine Parks. Ponderosa are often mixed with Rocky Mountain juniper, Douglas fir, and limber pine.

PONDEROSA CHARACTERISTICS

- Mature trees large, with open rounded or flat-topped crown.
- Height to 100 ft., trunk massive, to 3 ft. diameter
- Bark thick, reddish, with vanilla or butterscotch scent.
- Needles 3-7" long, in bundles of 2 to 3.
- Female cones large, woody, with a short spine on each scale.
- Trees scattered or in clumps, generally uncrowded.
- Diverse understory, dominated by shrubs and grasses.

PLANTS AND ANIMALS TO LOOK FOR:

Other Trees:
Douglas fir
Limber pine
Rocky Mountain juniper

Shrubs:
Antelope bitterbrush
Common juniper
Kinnikinnik
Mountain sagebrush
Wax currant

Reptiles and Amphibians:
Bullsnake
Eastern fence lizard

Wildflowers:
Blue grama grass
Golden aster
June-grass
Needle-and-thread
Sego lily
Spike fescue
Sulphur flower
Wyoming paintbrush

Mammals:
Abert's squirrel
Colorado chipmunk
Coyote
Golden-mantled ground
   squirrel
Mule deer
Nuttall's cottontail
Porcupine
Striped skunk

Birds:
Chipping sparrow
Dark-eyed junco
Mountain bluebird
Mountain chickadee
Northern Flicker
Steller's jay
Western tanager
White-breasted nuthatch
Yellow-rumped warbler

Butterflies:
Chryxus arctic
Common branded skipper
Dark wood nymph
Hoary elfin
Pine white
Thicket hairstreak
Western pine elfin

DOUGLAS FIR FORESTS

The forest of Douglas fir is cool, its floor darkened by the dense canopy above. The stillness invites quiet contemplation, until the chattering of a red squirrel echoes through the woods. The ground is covered with little more than needles, except where an opening in the trees admits precious sunlight to small shrubs and other understory plants. In such places, the bright yellow heads of arnica or goldenrod rise from the forest floor like dozens of little candles.

Forests of Douglas fir contrast sharply with nearby stands of ponderosa. Although both species reach their maximum size and numbers at lower elevations in the Rockies, the presence of Douglas fir signals a different environment than that of ponderosa. The Douglas fir occupies an intermediate but distinct ecological niche between dry ponderosa sites and cold, wet subalpine forests. Adjacent to Beaver Meadows, Moraine Park, and elsewhere at lower elevations in the park, Douglas fir prefer cool, moist north-facing slopes, opposite south-facing slopes where ponderosa grow. On intermediate sites, mixed forests of Douglas fir and ponderosa occur. At elevations above 9,000 feet, Douglas fir concentrate in warmer, south-facing locations, leaving the north-facing slopes to more cold-tolerant Engelmann spruce and subalpine fir.

Although they rarely attain the size of the gigantic Pacific Coast Douglas fir, the Rocky Mountain variety is similar in other respects. Narrow-topped crowns give them a Christmas-tree shape and their soft, blunt needles resemble those of true firs, such as the subalpine fir. Unlike the cones of true firs, which stand like candles at the top of the tree, Douglas fir cones grow throughout the crown and are one of the tree's most distinctive features. Three-pronged bracts project from between the woody scales, giving Douglas fir cones a shaggy appearance. The presence of these unique cones on the forest floor is a sure sign that a Douglas fir is near.

Douglas fir rarely form pure stands in the park. Usually, they mix with ponderosa, lodgepole pine, Engelmann spruce, subalpine fir, or aspen, depending on site conditions and past disturbance. Although understory vegetation is often sparse,

American kestrel (left);
Rocky Mountain maple leaves (below).

mountain maple, kinnikinnick, chokecherry, common juniper, fairy slipper orchids, false Solomon's seal, and twinflower commonly grow under Douglas fir. As in other dense conifer forests, diversity of plant species is relatively low.

Elk and mule deer, however, find Douglas fir forests good cover during the day. Their game trails crisscross the forests, tracing routes that lead to spring-greened meadows, where the animals browse in late afternoons, replenishing body fat lost during winter. Elk and deer also migrate through Douglas fir to and from summer range at higher elevations, feeding in meadows and riparian shrublands along the way.

The red squirrel, or chickaree, is a common resident of Douglas fir forests, where it piles up middens—collections of cone fragments often several feet deep and several yards across. Chickarees inhabit virtually all dense montane and subalpine forests, preferring these environments to ponderosa parklands. Highly territorial, these squirrels scold persistently when an intruder invades their space. When young leave the nests in mid-July, it is entertaining to watch the antics of these small versions of their parents learning how to be chickarees.

Southern red-backed voles, porcupines, snowshoe hares, ermine, and martens commonly inhabit Douglas fir forests as well as other dense stands of conifers. No bird species breed exclusively in Douglas fir, but birds typical of coniferous forests live here, including Steller's jays, white-breasted nuthatches, pine siskins, yellow-rumped warblers, dark-eyed juncos, red crossbills, and blue grouse.

During the mid-1980s, the majority of Douglas fir in the park were infested with spruce budworm, one of the most widespread insect diseases affecting conifers. The spruce budworm is the larva of a

Pine siskins

small orange-and-brown moth, which lays its eggs on the undersides of conifer needles. Upon hatching, the larvae spin webs in which they spend the winter. Come spring, the larvae move to the buds at the tips of twigs and feed on the tender new growth. They later develop into pupae and, within about a week,

Spruce budworm

metamorphose into adult moths to reproduce and renew the cycle.

Although spruce budworm infests other conifers, the epidemic was particularly noticeable among the park's Douglas fir stands, where tree mortality was more than 90 percent in some places. Such high mortality occurred as a result of a lengthy infestation. Budworms consumed new growth for several years, progressively reducing foliage, thus killing many trees.

Many agencies throughout the country control spruce budworm with pesticide sprays. The Park Service relies on natural controls—birds, predatory insects, parasites and extremely cold weather—to keep budworm in check. When the occasional epidemic does occur, budworms provide food for nuthatches, warblers, and other insect-eating birds. Dying trees become infested with bark beetles and other insects, which not only serve as an additional food source for many animals, but also begin to decompose the wood and recycle the trees' nutrients.

Trees eliminated by budworm and other disturbances open the forest canopy. Increased sunlight triggers the growth of wild raspberry, fireweed, wild rose, and other understory shrubs and herbaceous plants as well as occasional ponderosa and lodgepole pine seedlings. The forest ecosystem temporarily becomes more diverse and produces more forage for deer, elk, and other animals. These forest openings are usually short lived, however, as Douglas fir saplings poke through the herbaceous foliage and eventually restore the forest canopy.

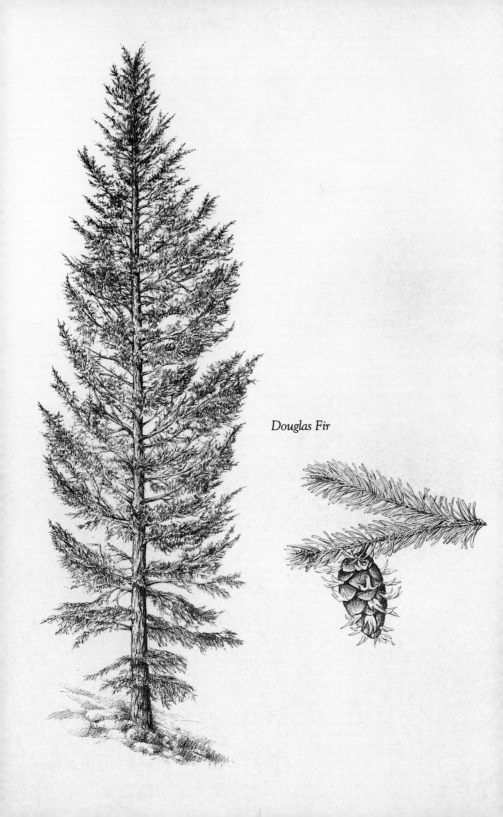

Douglas Fir

Douglas Fir Forests at a Glance

*D*ouglas fir forests are found on lower north-facing slopes in the park up to about 9,500 ft.. Rarely forming pure stands, Douglas fir are usually mixed with ponderosa pine, lodgepole pine, Engelmann spruce, and subalpine fir. Examples can be seen along the south sides of Horseshoe and Moraine Parks.

DOUGLAS FIR CHARACTERISTICS:

- Straight Christmas-tree shape with relatively dense foliage in crown.
- Height to approximately 100 ft., trunk diameter to 30".
- Needles 1" long, flat, with a rounded tip and a short stalk attaching them to the twig.
- Female cones 2" to 3" long, with prominent three-pronged papery bracts protruding from between the cone scales.
- Relatively dense stands.
- Sparse understory.

PLANTS AND ANIMALS TO LOOK FOR:

Shrubs:
Common juniper
Kinnikinnik
Mountain maple
Ninebark

Mammals:
Colorado chipmunk
Marten
Red squirrel (chickaree)
Snowshoe hare
Southern red-backed vole

Wildflowers:
Heart-leaved arnica
Pipsissewa
Smooth aster
Twisted stalk

Birds:
Brown creeper
Dark-eyed junco
Hermit thrush
Mountain chickadee
Pine siskin
Ruby-crowned kinglet
Steller's jay
White-breasted nuthatch

Woodnymph

LODGEPOLE PINE FORESTS

A stroll through a forest of lodgepole pine is like visiting a tree farm, so frequently are these stands of trees even-sized. American Indians favored young lodgepole as poles for tepees and other structures because they grow so tall and straight. In a lodgepole pine forest, ground vegetation is sparse, and unless the ground is littered with fallen trees, walking is easy. In moister places, myrtle blueberry carpets the forest floor, brightening the woods with its lime-green leaves. Hikers commonly see juniper, kinnikinnick, buffaloberry and, with eyes to the ground, coral root orchid, pipsissewa, woodnymph, and other floral jewels.

Lodgepole forests usually are quiet places, so pause for a few moments and listen to the subtle forest sounds: the soft "yanks" of white-breasted nuthatches, the slow, almost perfunctory warble of the yellow-rumped warbler, or the hurried cries of small flocks of pine sisken winging overhead. Dark-eyed juncos quietly flutter about on the ground, expertly picking seeds and insects from what appears to be a poorly stocked pantry. Mountain chickadees flit through the trees, calling to one another and often scolding intruders that enter their domain.

Chickarees are here, too, chattering, busily plucking cones from high branches, and foraging on the forest floor—but always watchful for predators, especially their archenemy, the marten. Martens are arboreal members of the weasel family that are almost as agile in the treetops as squirrels. Though mainly nocturnal, martens also hunt during the day. They show little fear of humans and often appear in campgrounds, much to the delight of park visitors. They linger, not for a handout, but for the opportunity to nab a

Marten

Lodgepole pine forest, Mummy Pass Trail

Colorado chipmunk, golden-mantled ground squirrel, or other unfortunate rodent that has become too fat and lazy from feeding on peanuts, popcorn, and other camp offerings.

In the Rocky Mountains, a lodgepole forest typically signifies drastic ecosystem disturbance. Lodgepole aggressively invade forests disturbed by logging, windfall, disease, landslides, road construction, and, especially, fire. Charcoal fragments, charred stumps, or fire scars at the bases of old trees confirm the fiery origin of a lodgepole forest. Common throughout the park, lodgepole stands of various ages are especially extensive in Kawuneeche Valley—testimony to a long history of fire.

Lodgepole pine are more adapted to fire than any other Rocky Mountain tree species. Their seedlings are especially tolerant of dry, sun-drenched, fire-scorched, ashy soils. The cones, unlike those of other Rocky Mountain conifers, may remain attached to the tree for decades. While some mature cones open to disperse seed, others remain closed, sealed by resin that protects viable seed, waiting for a fire. Fire burns many cones. For some, however, the fire's heat is just sufficient to destroy the resin seals yet not kill the seeds. When the fire dies, the

cones open, releasing seeds for a new forest.

Many people see forest fires as a symbol of destruction, killing wildlife and reducing magnificent forests to ashes. Actually, fires are a form of renewal. Old-growth Douglas fir and spruce-fir forests provide valuable habitat for certain species, but typically are less productive and diverse than younger forests. Fires return minerals to the soil that have accumulated in wood and set the stage for ecological succession. Above all, fires change plant communities, allowing greater diversity of plants and animals.

A walk through a forest area recently scarred by fire reveals how effective lodgepole regrowth can be, provided the species was present in the origi-

Young lodgepole in the aftermath of a fire.

nal forest. Within a few weeks, tiny lodgepole seedlings dot the ground, one of the first plants to grow among the ashes. During the following year, even more seedlings appear, as many as ten to a square foot. By this time, they are competing with other pioneers: wild raspberry, fireweed, wild rose, elderberry, grasses, and often aspen.

Once established, sun-loving lodgepole seedlings grow rapidly, as much as a foot per year in favorable sites. Soon, they overshadow and suppress herbs and shrubs, and may form an almost impenetrable stand of saplings, sometimes called "dog-hair stands." At this stage, it is a race for the sky. Lodgepoles do not like shade, and only the tallest, most vigorous trees survive. Their less competitive neighbors, trying vainly to reach the sun on weak, spindly stems, eventually succumb, sometimes arching over until their tops touch the ground. In this manner, the lodgepole stand is thinned and critical resources—light, nutrients, and moisture—are reapportioned to the strongest individuals.

Once the canopy matures, little direct sunlight reaches the forest floor, and lodgepole reproduction is effectively stopped. Only where wind or other causes topple trees, creating openings in the forest canopy, does

Porcupines live in all of the park's conifer ecosystems.

enough sunlight filter through to support lodgepole seedlings. Intermediate-aged stands of lodgepole often are filled with trees uniform in size and age. As stands become older, the addition of younger trees from such openings creates a less uniform forest.

Lodgepole almost always occur with other tree species for several reasons. First, fire and other disturbances rarely destroy all the trees in an area; the ones that remain serve as seed sources. Second, other species frequently become established along with lodgepole following a disturbance: aspen, ponderosa, limber pine, and Douglas fir at lower elevations; Engelmann spruce, subalpine fir, and limber pine at higher elevations. Third, natural forest succession usually favors shade-tolerant conifer seedlings. If their seeds are present, Douglas fir, Engelmann spruce, and subalpine fir will invade mature lodgepole stands. There are exceptions. At intermediate elevations, some lodgepole stands seem to remain stable under present climatic conditions. Most, however, gradually are overtaken by shade-tolerant conifers, which return the forest to a climax state.

Fireweed blooms in a burned lodgepole forest.

Lodgepole PIne

*L*arge stands of lodgepole pine are found throughout the park, and usually indicate areas that were burned within the last century or two. Look for burned stumps, or fragments of charcoal half buried in the soil. Extensive stands of various ages grow on both sides of Kawuneeche Valley, along the upper half of the Bear Lake Road, and along the road to the Wild Basin ranger station.

LODGEPOLE CHARACTERISTICS:

- Trees in dense stands are tall and straight, with narrow crowns; in open sites, their crown is broader, resembling ponderosa.
- Height to approximately 90 ft., trunk diameter to 18".
- Needles 1" to 2" long in bundles of two; more of a yellow-green color than those of other conifers.
- Female cones up to 2" long, many remaining closed and attached to the tree for many years.

- Stands often appearing even-aged, with most of the trees about the same size.
- Usually sparse understory.
- Trees in younger stands often nearly all lodgepole; older stands invaded by shade-tolerant spruce, subalpine fir, or Douglas fir.

PLANTS AND ANIMALS TO LOOK FOR:

Shrubs:
Broom huckleberry
Common juniper
Kinnikinnik
Scouler willow
Buffaloberry
Sticky laurel

Mammals:
Marten
Porcupine
Red squirrel
Southern red-backed vole

Wildflowers:
Blue clematis
Dwarf mistletoe
Fairy slipper
Heart-leaved arnica
Lesser wintergreen
One-sided wintergreen
Pinedrops

Birds:
Dark-eyed junco
Gray jay
Hermit thrush
Mountain chickadee
Red crossbill
Ruby-crowned kinglet
White-breasted nuthatch
Yellow-rumped warbler

Aspen along Glacier Creek.

ASPEN GROVES

Aspens are four-season trees. Their new, light-green foliage brightens in spring, becomes darker in summer, then bursts into blazons of yellows, oranges, and reds in autumn. Their velvety smooth bark ranges from bone white to pale greens and oranges, punctuated with black scars that seem to peer from the grove like a multitude of eyes. Regardless of season, the colors of aspen groves set them apart from the deep greens of surrounding conifers. Even in winter, when the last, quivering leaves have dropped from the branches and the groves are

Aspen trees in spring; male evening grosbeak (inset).

cold, windy, and seemingly lifeless, they stand in stark, gray contrast to the dark forms of pine, spruce, and fir.

In late spring and early summer, aspen groves bustle with birds. Park visitors can hear house wrens' loud, bouncy songs, the soft cooing of mountain bluebirds, the nasal calls of western wood pewees, and the insistent rapping of red-naped sapsuckers and downy woodpeckers as they drum on dead branches or hollow out nest holes. Tree and violet-green swallows wheel and dive, and robins search eagerly for earthworms.

Aspen forests and groves, which often border meadows such as Horseshoe Park and Moraine Park, are productive places. Each autumn, the fallen leaves of these deciduous trees, along with those of numerous understory plants, attract a host of hungry soil insects and other invertebrates. The leaf fragments and feces they leave are further decomposed by bacteria and fungi. This process recycles mineral nutrients from the leaves and produces humus from the decomposed organic material. These substances enrich the soil, resulting in a prolific and diverse understory that differs markedly from the relatively sparse growth under nearby conifers.

Colorado columbine.

In drier sites, the understory of aspen groves is usually dominated by grasses; in wetter sites, by shrubs such as chokecherry, gooseberry, snowberry, wild rose, and mountain maple. Wildflowers are abundant. White geranium has a particular affinity for aspen groves, as does Fendler meadowrue and aspen daisy. Aspen groves are good places to look for Colorado columbine and purple-flowered lupine. Often, the air is filled with the sweet smell of northern bedstraw's tiny white flowers.

This copious vegetation attracts numbers of animals seeking food, shelter, and denning or nesting sites. Birds nest in tree cavities that woodpeckers have hollowed in the soft aspen wood. Some trees are veritable apartment houses, with families of swallows, house wrens, bluebirds, and sapsuckers, each occupying a separate hole. One of the most common birds is the warbling vireo, which usually builds its nest in the fork of an aspen branch. Although their rolling warble is heard almost constantly while they are on the nest, these vireos seem impossible to spot.

Warbling vireo chicks

On the ground, montane and long-tailed voles, deer mice and western jumping mice, chipmunks, and golden-mantled ground squirrels make their homes among understory plants. Cottontail rabbits build warrens under shrubs along the edges of aspen groves. Although northern pocket gophers are rarely seen, the mounds of soil they push out of their tunnels each night are everywhere. All of these small mammals attract coyotes, red foxes, ermine, long-tailed weasels, shrews, and other predators. Shrews, the smallest of mammals, are voracious feeders because of their high metabolic rate. Most of their diet consists of insects and other invertebrates, and each day they must eat more than their own body weight.

Mule deer and elk, seeking cover and forage, frequent aspen groves. Groves with dense, tall understory shrubs make especially good nurseries for cow elk during calving time. If browse is scarce in an elk herd's winter range and aspen are present, elk often gnaw the bark, frequently girdling and killing trees. Elk-destroyed aspen habitat is visible in Horseshoe Park, Beaver Meadows, and other low elevations in the park.

The aspen species found in the park is called quaking aspen, so named because its leaves vibrate or tremble in the slightest breeze. The most widely distributed native tree in North America, quaking aspen grows at all elevations in the park up to timberline, although it is primarily a tree of montane and lower subalpine forests. Aspen, cottonwoods, and other poplars are in the willow family. Like willows, aspen flowers are borne on catkins. Like cottonwood seeds, each tiny aspen seed has a tuft of hair that allows wind to transport it over long distances.

Tree swallows nest exclusively in tree cavities, usually in aspen (right). Fall aspen colors (below).

Although aspen do reproduce by seed, requirements for germination and seedling survival are apparently so exacting that this type of reproduction is rare. Fortunately for the aspen, its ability to propagate from its root system is robust.

Once an aspen is established in a favorable site, its lateral roots produce vertical shoots, called suckers. Some of the suckers eventually reach the size of mature trees. Over time, a group of trees results, all interconnected by a single root system. Recent research in Utah suggests that an aspen grove in that state may be the world's most massive—and oldest—organism. Growing from a root system that has apparently continued producing trees for thousands of years, the present grove of interconnected aspens weighs more than 13 million pounds.

Because vegetative propagation produces trees that are genetically identical, the group of trees is called a clone. The trees look similar and behave similarly, producing leaves at the same time in spring and changing leaf color at the same time in fall. Usually clone trees are the same sex, have the same bark color, and have similar resistance to certain diseases. Although an aspen grove might consist of more than one clone, the separate clones often can be distinguished. In spring, some clones produce leaves earlier than others; in autumn, differences between each clone's leaf colors become apparent.

As the clone matures, suckering declines in the dense center of the grove and becomes restricted to peripheral locations where soil conditions are favorable and sunlight is abundant. Apparently mature trees in the center of the grove produce hormones that suppress suckering. Suckering can resume if the large trees are eliminated by elk damage, disease, windfall, logging, or other causes.

Because aspen improve the soil and provide a protected environment, shade-tolerant conifers typically invade and eventually replace them if conifer seed sources are available. Along with lodgepole pine, aspen are usually pioneer plants in disturbed areas, and are considered a successional species. Aspen frequently populate burned areas, often sprouting from roots that have survived the fire, forming a pure stand or one mixed with lodgepole and other conifers. In avalanche paths, frequent avalanches may eliminate most conifers, thus favoring a long-lived aspen community. Stable aspen stands also may occur in places where soil moisture is too high for conifers, yet within the tolerance range of aspen.

Scarred aspen result from elk gnawing the nutrient-rich bark in early spring.

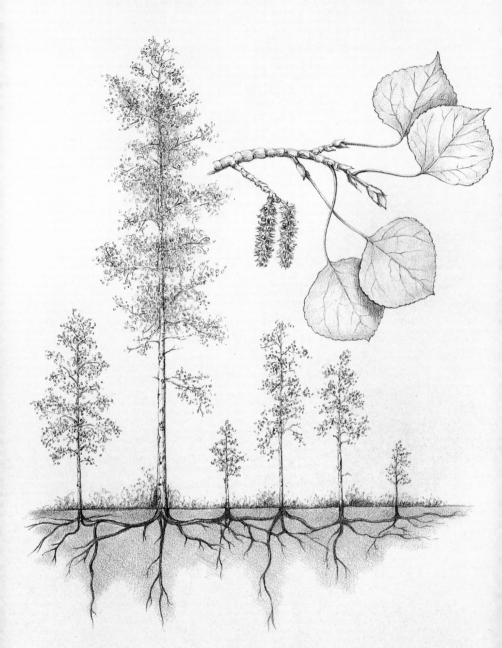

Aspen groves consist of one or more clones. A clone forms when the roots of a parent aspen produce new shoots, called suckers. Each sucker may become a tree. All the trees of a clone are united by a common root system and are actually a single organism!

Aspen Groves at a Glance

A spen are widely distributed throughout the park below 10,000 ft, and less commonly at higher elevations up to treeline. Look for aspen around the margins of meadows and stream valleys, but they are found in a variety of other sites where fire, avalanches, or other disturbance has removed the original conifer forest.

ASPEN CHARACTERISTICS:

- Broad, oval, leaves with thin, flattened stem allowing leaf to quiver or tremble in the slightest of breezes.
- Smooth, light-colored bark ranging from bone white to tan or greenish, with numerous black or brown branch scars, cankers, and other blemishes.
- Often grow in clumps or groves

- Lush understory compared to conifer forests
- Older groves usually invaded by young conifers.
- The only common deciduous tree growing on mountain slopes away from riparian zones.

PLANTS AND ANIMALS TO LOOK FOR:

Shrubs:
Chokecherry
Common gooseberry
Common juniper
Serviceberry
Snowberry
Wild rose

Mammals:
Masked shrew
Montane shrew
Montane vole
Northern pocket gopher
Western jumping mouse

Wildflowers:
Aspen daisy
Colorado columbine
Fendler meadowrue
Northern bedstraw
Silvery lupine
White geranium
Yarrow

Butterflies:
Dreamy dusky-wing
 skipper
Weidemeyer's admiral
Western tiger swallowtail

Birds:
Cordilleran flycatcher
Downy woodpecker
Hairy woodpecker
House wren
Mountain bluebird
Red-naped sapsucker
Tree swallow
Violet-green swallow
Warbling vireo

SUBALPINE FORESTS
ENGELMANN SPRUCE–SUBALPINE FIR FORESTS

Above the realm of ponderosa and Douglas fir, the character of the forest changes. Here, along the slopes of peaks and higher ridges, the tall spire-like crowns of Engelmann spruce and subalpine fir crowd together to form a nearly unbroken band of dense forest that extends the length of the southern Rockies. Cold and moist, these forests are reminiscent of those in boreal regions.

At their lower margins, between 8,000 and 9,500 feet, spruce-fir forests are interspersed with stands of ponderosa pine, lodegepole pine, Douglas fir, and aspen, often forming extensive mixed forests with these species. The upper margins of spruce-fir forests extend to treeline, above which cold temperatures and short growing seasons prevent tree growth. In between, Engelmann spruce and subalpine fir dominate all but the most arid and rocky sites.

Spruce-fir forests, such as found below Specimen Mountain near Milner Pass, are snowy places in winter, with average snow depths often exceeding five feet. Such accumulations result from the normally heavier precipitation at higher elevations and because strong winter winds blow much of the snow from above treeline into the subalpine forest. Some forest snowdrifts linger into late spring or early summer. In places, forest soils are saturated with meltwater during much of the summer. In fact, precipitation in subalpine forests typically is high year-round.

Abundant moisture produces a greater understory on the spruce-fir forest floor than is found in dense stands of other conifers. Blueberry and broom huckleberry usually carpet the ground and clumps of currant, common juniper, bush honeysuckle, and elderberry are common. Late spring brings the delicate pink blossoms of fairy slipper orchids. During summer, the pink blooms of fireweed, yellow arnica, and the blue flowers of chiming bells and Jacob's ladder abound. Twinflower bears its

Spruce-fir forest in Paradise Park.

dainty, pink blossoms in pairs atop small stalks that rise from tiny vines. Yet, this fragrant flower is often overlooked because of its small size.

Subalpine spruce-fir forests are considered climax ecosystems, with Engelmann spruce and subalpine fir usually replacing lodgepole and aspen below an elevation of about 10,000 feet. Above that, spruce and fir either reseed directly or replace limber pine that have colonized a disturbed area. Natural reforestation at higher sites can take a long time. For example, the burn on Jackstraw Mountain, viewed from Trail Ridge Road just below Milner Pass, supports only a sparse population of small spruces and firs. They grow among a jumble of charred spruce trunks killed by a 1871 forest fire.

Hiking through an old-growth forest, deep in the shadow of trees that have stood for perhaps four or five centuries, a visitor senses the primeval. The air is damp and the ground is so moist and soft that footsteps barely make a sound. A rich, earthy smell pervades the forest. Standing amid thick tree trunks and looking skyward, we are often hard-pressed to distinguish one crown from another, so much do their boughs intermingle. And all around, shade-tolerant saplings of the next generation grow among shrubs and fallen trees, some day to take their place among the forest giants.

These high, dense forests are the natural habitat of wolverine and lynx, although few, if any, of these solitary predators remain in the park. More likely, you will see marten, long-tailed weasel, ermine, and, occasionally, black bear. Chickaree, least chipmunks, red-backed voles, and snowshoe hare (shown at left) are all common, as are mule deer and elk, which browse meadows and margins at dawn and dusk but rest in the forest during the day.

Because of the dense forest canopy, you are more likely to hear birds than see them. Although birds of other conifer forests frequent spruce-fir forests, several species are particularly common among the spruces and firs. Perhaps one of the most beautiful voices heard in the Rockies

A spruce stump in Paradise Park; chickaree, or red squirrel (inset).

belongs to the hermit thrush. Singing from atop a tall tree, the thrushes clear, flute-like song seems to float over the forest. More commonly heard are the bouncy warbles of the ruby-crowned kinglet and scolding mountain chickadees. One species that breeds almost exclusively in spruce-fir stands is the pine grosbeak. These relatively tame, large finches often are seen feeding on the ground, seemingly oblivious to nearby hikers.

The character of the spruce-fir forest changes near treeline. Forest openings become more common and trees become shorter. Their tops often have such a windswept, one-sided appearance that they are known as "flag" or "banner" trees. At these elevations, spruce and fir also tend to propagate by "layering." This phenomenon occurs when a lower branch rests on the ground and produces roots. One or more twigs on this rooted horizontal branch become dominant, forming vertical shoots that develop into a tree. Numerous spruce and fir at high elevations have "skirts" of smaller daughter trees produced by layering.

*Near treeline on Trail Ridge (above);
a white-crowned sparrow (left).*

The upper margins of subalpine forests are fragmented into tree islands called krummholz, a German word meaning "crooked wood." Here, at the transition between forest and tundra, the effects of wind, cold temperatures, and winter's scouring, windborne ice crystals produce stunted, malformed trees that bear little resemblance to those growing farther below. At treeline, around 11,400 feet, trees are close to their limits of growth, and grow very slowly. Individuals with trunks only a few inches in diameter may be several hundred years old.

Tree islands range from large, ragged looking stands with many one-sided flag trees to small mounds resembling shrubs. Where winds are strong, the islands often grow in the protected lee of boulders and display sculptured, streamlined shapes. Tree islands begin with the germination of a seed, usually behind a boulder, shrub, small mound of turf, or in other places protected from the wind. As the tree grows, it reproduces by layering its downwind branches. The result is a cluster of small trees. Unless protected by a boulder, the windward portion of the tree island gradually dies while the downwind part continues to grow. Over decades, the tree island may actually creep downwind. Most tree islands consist of Engelmann spruce, subalpine fir, or a mix of the two. Limber pines also grow at treeline, but because they are normally incapable of branch layering, they stand as solitary, often grotesquely twisted sentinels.

Because the krummholz zone forms a transition between forest and tundra, the diversity of plant species is relatively high. Here, alpine wildflowers, such as American bistort and alpine avens, mix with Jacob's ladder and other subalpine species. During the summer, deer and elk frequent krummholz areas where trees provide cover and the intervening meadows offer abundant forage. White-crowned sparrows are one of the most common breeding birds in the krummholz. Their loud, clear songs echo across the cirque basins and tundra slopes of their spectacular mountain home.

Longs Peak and Pagoda Mountain viewed from Glacier Gorge.

Engelmann Spruce

Spruce-Fir Forests at a Glance

*F*orests composed mainly of Engelmann spruce and subalpine fir form an almost unbroken band of timber at higher elevations from about 9,500 ft. to treeline. Good examples can be seen just below treeline along upper Fall River Road and Trail Ridge Road.

ENGELMANN SPRUCE CHARACTERISTICS:

- Straight trunk and dense crown having a narrow conical shape.

- Height to approximately 100 ft., trunk diameter to 30".

- Needles attached singly to twig, about 1" long, 4-sided, with sharp tip.

- Bark in plate-like layers, relatively thin, reddish on protected side of tree, otherwise gray.

- Female cones 1" to 2" long with very papery scales, tan to reddish, mostly clustered in upper third of tree.

- Thick forests of tall trees with narrow crowns and a dark green color, appearing from afar as a dark band on mountain slopes just below treeline.

- Upper forest margins ragged and fragmented into wind-sculpted tree islands.

- Understory more dense than other conifer forest types except ponderosa stands; immature spruces and firs usually abundant.

PLANTS AND ANIMALS TO LOOK FOR:

Shrubs:
Broom huckleberry
Colorado currant
Common juniper
Myrtle blueberry
Wild raspberry

Mammals:
Least chipmunk
Long-tailed weasel
Masked shrew
Porcupine
Red squirrel
Snowshoe hare
Southern red-backed vole

Wildflowers:
Curled lousewort
Broad-leaved arnica
Fairy slipper
Heart-leaved arnica
Jacob's ladder
Pipsissewa
Red columbine
Twinflower
Woodnymph
Wooton senecio

Birds:
Blue grouse
Dark-eyed junco
Golden-crowned kinglet
Hermit thrush
Mountain chickadee
Olive-sided flycatcher
Pine grosbeak
Ruby-crowned kinglet
Townsend's solitaire
Yellow-rumped warbler

Subalpine Fir

SUBALPINE FIR CHARACTERISTICS:

- *Crown often narrower, more spire-like than Engelmann spruce; foliage extremely dense.*

- *Height to approximately 80 ft., trunk diameter to 28".*

- *Needles attached singly to twig, flat, with rounded tips and soft to the touch; often arc upward so that the tips point skyward.*

- *Bark typically thin, smooth, and silvery, with horizontal markings; shallow vertical furrows common on older bark.*

- *Female cones purplish, often glistening with pitch, and growing upright, candlelike on uppermost branches of the tree. Cones usually disintegrate while on the tree, so are rarely found on the ground unless removed by squirrels.*

LIMBER PINE WOODLANDS

Tenacious and resilient, limber pines cling to rocky outcrops and exposed ridges where water is scant and soils are thin. These bent, misshapen trees somehow survive howling winds and arctic temperatures in places inhospitable to any other type of tree in the park. Although limber pine commonly grow with other conifers at lower elevations, they seem to thrive best in the subalpine environments, often forming pure stands near treeline. Their rounded or flat-topped appearance contrasts with the tall, pointed crowns of spruce and fir. Slopes forested with limber pine appear woolly when seen from a distance.

The limber pine gets its name from its unusually flexible branches, which bend rather than break in the high mountain winds. It also grows a strong taproot that penetrates fractures in the bedrock, firmly anchoring the tree as well as reaching water unavailable at the surface. These characteristics help the tree endure—and thrive—in rigorous subalpine climates.

Related to white pines, the limber produces needles in groups of five, compared with clusters of two and three for ponderosa and two for lodgepole. Like its close relative, the piñon pine, the limber pine produces small, wingless seeds—called nuts—that are a favorite food of rodents and birds, especially the Clark's nutcracker.

A limber pine remnant on Trail Ridge.

Clark's nutcrackers—black, white, and gray birds a little larger than robins—belong to the jay family. They are common in park campgrounds, picnic areas, and observation pullouts along Trail Ridge Road. Apart from their panhandling habits, nutcrackers play a major role in the ecology of the limber pine.

When the large, woody cones of the limber pine ripen in the fall, nutcrackers pry open the cone scales with their long, sturdy bills and extract the nuts. The nutcracker then evaluates the nut's worth by assessing its weight or the sound that it makes as the bird rattles the nut with its bill. The bird either discards the nut or places it in a pouch under its tongue. The pouch can hold numerous nuts, permitting the bird to forage over large areas. Most of the nuts are hidden in caches the bird digs in the soil. The nutritious nuts provide an important winter food source for breeding adult nutcrackers as well as an energy- and protein-rich staple in the diet of nestlings.

Far more nuts are hidden than are recovered by birds, however, and many unrecovered ones germinate. Because germination requires that a viable seed be covered by the proper amount of soil in a protected location, nuts buried by nutcrackers have a much greater chance of germination than those that merely fall from cones. Pines with multiple trunks are often several trees that grew from a seed cache.

Alpine actinea (left);
least chipmunk (above).

The understory in limber pine woodlands is sparse compared to other forest types in the park. Common shrubs include kinnikinnick, common juniper, waxflower, and blueberry. Spotted saxifrage, stonecrop, dwarf goldenrod, and cutleaf erigeron are among the wildflowers frequently found under the pines, along with purple reedgrass, a grass common to dry, subalpine soils.

The dominant role of limber pine in exposed sites near treeline is unusual for the southern Rocky Mountains. In central Colorado and southward, they either share dominance with bristlecone pine or are absent at higher elevations. In northern Wyoming, whitebark pine is the typical treeline species in exposed locations. Only in northern Colorado (including Rocky Mountain National Park) and southern Wyoming does it appear that the absence of these other species allows limber pine to dominate dry, rocky, high-elevation sites.

Limber pine also play an important role in reforesting disturbed areas. Above the range of lodgepole and aspen, limber pine are the predominant pioneer species in areas disturbed by fire, disease, avalanches, and other causes. Seldom forming pure stands in these places, it is mixed with Engelmann spruce and subalpine fir as well as a few aspen and lodgepole. Eventually, limber pine is replaced by spruce and fir in all but the driest sites.

WHY **NOT** TO FEED WILDLIFE

Feeding wildlife is discouraged by the Park Service for several reasons:

1. Feeding brings animals in closer contact with people, causing the animals to lose their fear of humans; this is potentially dangerous for both animals and people—wild animals bite and often carry disease.

2. Animals may develop a dependence on food from humans, plentiful during summer, but non-existent during winter; this may hasten their starvation or make them more susceptible to predation.

3. Feeding animals may disrupt the ecosystem in ways that aren't readily apparent. In the case of Clark's nutcrackers, feeding panhandling birds could alter seed-burying habits of the birds, and be detrimental to limber pine regeneration.

So when you are in the park, enjoy the wildlife, but please don't offer food.

Limber Pine

Although common at treeline, limber pine are found many places in the park at lower elevations. They are usually mixed with other conifer species, but do occur in a few relatively pure stands, especially on sites that are rocky and exposed to the wind. There are many stands growing alongside Trail Ridge Road between Many Parks Curve and treeline.

- Sparse, often scraggly appearing forest.
- Typical of wind-exposed rocky ridges at or below treeline.
- Understory usually limited to a few shrubs or herbaceous plants growing in rock crevices or on small accumulations of soil.

LIMBER PINE CHARACTERISTICS:

- Gnarled and twisted in windy sites; in more protected areas, crown broad, symmetrical and often flat-topped.
- Typically a small tree, 15-30 ft. tall, with a trunk diameter to 18"; trees frequently with multiple trunks.
- Older bark gray and platelike; thin and smooth on younger branches, often with pinkish color at windy sites.

- Needles 1" to 2" long in bundles of four or five.
- Female cones large, often several inches long with thick, woody scales; cones bear seeds approximately 3/8" long in fall.

PLANTS AND ANIMALS TO LOOK FOR:

Shrubs:
Broom huckleberry
Common juniper
Kinnikinnik
Shrubby cinquefoil
Buffaloberry
Sticky laurel

Mammals:
Deer mouse
Ermine
Golden-mantled ground squirrel
Least chipmunk
Nuttall's cottontail
Red squirrel
Yellow-bellied marmot

Wildflowers:
Common alum-root
Golden whitlow-wort
Mountain candytuft
Spotted saxifrage
Stonecrop
Whipple's penstemon

Birds:
Clark's nutcracker
Common raven
Dark-eyed junco
Gray jay
Mountain chickadee
Pine siskin
Yellow-rumped warbler

ALPINE TUNDRA

Above the realm of trees lies alpine tundra—an enchanting, windswept world of contrasts. Here, no trees obscure the line where ridge and sky meet, and mountaintops stand out sharply against the sky. Thousand-foot headwalls of glacial cirques abruptly cut gently rounded tundra slopes, providing eagle's-eye views of valleys below. Some alpine areas are covered with grassy meadows or lush carpets of wildflowers, while others appear rocky and barren, or are cloaked by snowfields. In winter, vicious winds tear at the vegetation, claw at the rocks, and drive razor-sharp ice crystals at anything in their path. Yet, summer breezes can be so gentle that they barely raise the hair on the back of a marmot basking on a sunny boulder. In alpine tundra, the extremes of mountain climate seem pronounced.

Tundra vegetation is short. Some plants are so tiny that you have to crouch on hands and knees to find them. At first glance, the vegetation may appear monotonous. Take another look. A slight rise in the ground here, a little furrow there, some wet ground below a snowbank in another place—each such site sports a different plant community. The closer you look, the more the tundra becomes a mosaic of different communities, nature's version of a patchwork quilt. Slight differences in soil moisture, winter snow cover, and wind exposure encourage some plant species while discouraging others. Even extremely rocky or barren places have at least a few plants growing on them.

On alpine tundra, spring arrives first to places where winds have swept the ground free of snow. Pink-and-white springbeauties peek out from rosettes of burgundy-colored leaves, tiny

Big-rooted springbeauty.

white mountain candytuft and rockjasmine flowers decorate gravelly fellfield soils, and purple, dime-sized fairy primroses hide in still-brown patches of turf.

Soon, melting snows are replaced by bright green meadows. By mid-summer, the tundra has exploded in a glorious display of floral fireworks. Yellows of alpine avens, actinea, and rydbergia mix with purple sky-pilots, blue harebells and chiming bells, and the deep reds of king's crown. White and yellow marsh marigolds festoon the margins of tundra ponds while, nearby, magenta clusters of Parry's primrose suffuse the air with their heavy fragrance.

Arctic gentian.

In August, greenish-white arctic gentian flowers signify the waning of the brief tundra summer. By then, another show of colors has begun. Summer's green leaves rapidly change to warm autumn tones as if to offset the nip in the air. By mid-September, brilliant ruby, garnet, and topaz shades of alpine avens and other plants blend with more subtle auburn, copper, and ocher hues in a spectacle that rivals the changing colors of aspen a few thousand feet below. All has changed again by the middle of November. Several storms have already lashed the mountaintops and snowdrifts have closed Trail Ridge Road for another winter season. A new blanket of snow covers the tundra, and what vegetation remains has turned a tawny brown.

Tundra is a word of Russian origin meaning "land without trees." Although tundra occurs mostly in cold, arctic latitudes, the southern Rockies and other mountain regions have arctic-like climates at higher elevations. We refer to these areas as alpine tundra.

Alpine and arctic tundra around the world share many of the same plant species. Wildflowers such as alpine speedwell and mountain dryad, for example, are found in Rocky Mountain National Park as well as in arctic Asia. Species such as dwarf columbine and rydbergia, however, are found only in the Rocky Mountains, apparently having evolved here.

Nearly a third of the park is above treeline, making the park one of the largest expanses of alpine tundra preserved by the National Park Service in the contiguous states. Trail Ridge Road provides millions of people access to the tundra each year. Despite such numbers, the vegetation is in remarkably good condition. Unlike many other alpine areas in the southern Rockies, the park has experienced little sheep grazing or other livestock use, which can alter and degrade plant communities. In fact, the pristine quality of the tundra, together with its vastness, were key factors in the United Nations' designation of Rocky Mountain National Park as an international biosphere reserve.

Tundra, whether arctic or alpine, is determined by severe climatic conditions. A rule of thumb is that tundra is found where the average temperature of the warmest month (July in the southern Rockies) is 50 degrees Fahrenheit or less. Mean annual temperatures in tundra are below freezing, and the effective growing season is too cool and short to support trees. Because atmosphere is thinner at higher elevations, solar radiation is more intense. In addition, average annual precipitation above treeline in the Front Range is typically about 40 inches, with more than half of it falling as snow.

Wind is another factor. Summer visitors cannot fully appreciate the extreme severity of wind on alpine tundra. A 1974 study conducted on Trail Ridge measured an average wind speed of 30 miles per hour from January through May, with maximum gusts exceeding 100 miles per hour (hurricane-force winds are 74 miles per hour or greater). Wind speeds are high even during summer. The average speed measured at the Alpine Tundra Museum during the summer of 1980 was 20 miles per hour, with gusts nearing 80 miles per hour. Researchers maintained an anemometer on top of Longs Peak during the winter of 1981, and the instrument recorded a gust of 201 miles per hour, over twice hurricane force. Because high elevations are almost always windy, a calm 60-degree summer afternoon on alpine tundra is a rare treat to be enjoyed.

How do tundra plants survive these climatic challenges? An obvious adaptation is short stature. Uneven terrain and vegetation slow winds dramatically near the ground, so that a layer of relatively calm air lies just above the soil even on the windiest days. Scientists call this a boundary layer. The sun heats soil, rocks, and vegetation, which, in turn, warm the air in the boundary layer, creating a microclimate that may be 20 to 30 degrees warmer than air just a few feet above. You can experience this effect by lying flat on the ground during a windy day. If tundra plants stay short enough to remain within the boundary layer, their growing conditions are not as bad as might be expected.

Locations more exposed to the wind have a thinner boundary layer and shorter plants. Moss campion and many other plants that live in such places form low-growing cushions or mats that look like moss. But when moss campion blooms, its profusion of pink blossoms nearly conceals its tiny leaves, clearly telling us that it is definitely not a moss.

Another adaptation of tundra plants is their ability to grow and reproduce at lower temperatures than other flora. Tiny blue-and-yellow alpine forget-me-nots, for example, often grow on windy sites that remain snow-free most of the winter. Yet, severe conditions do not stop these May-blooming heralds of spring, and an early start seems just reward for enduring winter's hardship without a protective blanket of snow.

Other tundra communities must wait until their snow cover melts before substantial growth occurs. When growth does begin, it is with a flourish. Shoots grow rapidly, and many species produce flowers before leaves are fully developed. Snowbank buttercup, one of the most rapid bloomers, frequently produces bright yellow patches of flowers only inches from the melting edges of snowbanks.

Such rapid growth and flower production are partly the results of large root masses. Nearly all tundra plants are perennials, which means they live for several years—in some cases decades—allowing the growth of large taproots, bulbs, tubers, and other root structures. Big-rooted springbeauty, for example, has a fleshy taproot that reaches down six feet or more into soils and rock crevices. During summer, much of the

Alpine phlox and alpine avens; snowbank buttercup (right).

sugars and other substances produced by photo-
synthesis is transported to the root for storage.
When the following spring arrives, these energy resources rapidly move out of the root into
the developing shoot, enabling fast growth and
flower production in a growing season that may
last only six weeks. Scientific studies of herbaceous plant communities in Colorado alpine tundra have found that
root structures generally account for more than 90 percent of the living
plant biomass.

Snowstorms frequently occur in July or August on the alpine tundra, to
the disdain of many visitors. Such events would quickly arrest plant
growth at lower elevations, but tundra plants have adapted. They
thrive in cool climates and benefit from the added moisture.

Even leaf colors can be adaptive. Many tundra plants produce leaves
that, at times, are more red than green. The red, purple, or bluish colors

of immature leaves and stems result from the pigment anthocyanin. Researchers believe this pigment protects plants from tissue-damaging ultraviolet radiation by absorbing and transforming some of the radiation into heat. As tissues mature and chlorophyll is produced, the reddish colors are masked by green. Chlorophyll production diminishes as fall approaches, and anthocyanin as well as pigments such as xanthophyll and carotene produce striking autumn colors.

Another form of environmental adaptation are the fine hairs that cover the leaves of many alpine plants. These hairs not only reflect excess radiation, but also moderate against water loss caused by desiccating winds. A fuzzy covering of hair may also trap heat, like a miniature greenhouse. Buds of the black-headed daisy and other species are covered with dark hairs that absorb radiation better than white hairs, and may help to warm the flower developing inside.

In an environment where early snows, unusually wet summers, and other weather vagaries make seed production unreliable, tundra plants often depend on vegetative reproduction. Besides requiring less energy than the flowering process, vegetative reproduction is often quicker and more effective in colonizing open ground. Many plants reproduce vegetatively by growing additional shoots from root structures. Others, like the whiplash saxifrage, mimic strawberries by sending runners over the ground that sprout little plants at their tips when they reach favorable soil. The alpine bistort produces tiny bulblets on its stem—minuscule plants ready to grow as soon as they fall to the ground.

One aspect of tundra ecology of special interest to the Park Service is disturbance. Although the agency is especially concerned about the effects of large numbers of visitors, other factors cause disturbance, too. Burrowing animals such as chipmunks, marmots, and especially pocket gophers break up turf, and heavy use by elk and bighorn causes disturbance in some areas. Once the plant cover is broken, wind and water erosion may increase the area and severity of damage.

While tundra plants are well adapted to their environment, the severe climate drastically limits vegetation's ability to recover from disturbance. Recovery may take decades, even centuries, depending on location and degree of damage. One botanist, Dr. Beatrice Willard, has been studying vegetation in disturbed areas of the park for more than 30 years. She found, for example, that a cushion plant community required two decades to recover from a single summer of human foot

Red king's crown, yellow alpine avens, and white American bistort grow among boulders (right).

Fairy primrose along the Ute Trail (below).

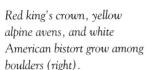

traffic. Willard also estimated that it takes severely damaged kobresia sedge turf 500 to 1,000 years to recover.

In 1935, the old Fall River Road west of the Alpine Tundra Museum was closed with completion of the present road over Trail Ridge. The old roadbed was torn up and the slopes restored to approximate conditions before the road existed. Since then, natural revegetation has taken place on the strip of bare soil that once marked the old route. From a distance, it is difficult to tell that a road was there. As you walk the hiking trail that now follows the route down to Milner Pass, however, the new vegetation along this strip still clearly differs from surrounding plant communities, six decades later.

Because tundra plants are so susceptible to trampling, the Park Service has established three tundra protection areas on Trail Ridge: the Tundra Nature Trail to the Toll Memorial that starts at the Rock Cut parking area, the trail to Forest Canyon Overlook, and the trail that climbs to the knob immediately north of the Alpine Tundra Museum parking lot. In these areas, people must stay on established trails. Failure to do so warrants a citation. The public can walk on tundra in all other areas, but park staff ask that visitors take the following precautions to help minimize impact: rock hop wherever possible to reduce the number of plants trampled; when walking in groups, spread out rather than walk in single file; and simply watch where you place your feet to reduce visible impact on the plants.

Tundra is fascinating in its own right, but it is also a good place to watch wildlife. Although fewer animal species are found here than in any other ecosystem in the park, many are readily seen because of the lack of cover. Elk, bighorn sheep, and mule deer are abundant during the summer. Marmots and pikas almost always can be found in rocky areas, and one might see a coyote, a long-tailed weasel, or a porcupine crossing the tundra. You are more apt to spot larger wildlife early in the morning or late in the afternoon. Smaller animals are active later in the morning when it is sunny and temperatures are warmer. Binoculars are a handy accessory. When not using them to view wildlife or distant peaks, you can reverse them and use them as a hand lens to study insects or plant parts.

The tundra climate limits animal activity. Although pikas, ptarmigan, and a few other species remain, most birds and many mammals migrate to lower elevations during the winter. Because insects and other invertebrates are generally sluggish until the sun warms the tundra, their life cycles may stretch to two or more years instead of a few weeks or months typical at lower elevations. Leafhoppers, scarab beetles, crab and wolf spiders, and mites are present on the tundra. Picnickers should take note that, in spite of the climate, a half-dozen kinds of ants are on hand to claim their share of lunch.

Flies are important pollinators on the tundra, primarily because they can fly at lower temperatures than bees can. Although fewer bees live in tundra areas than in lower ecosystems, the hum of bumblebees making their rounds from flower to flower is commonplace in the high country. When the air is cool, bumblebees can raise their body temperatures by rapidly vibrating their wing muscles—a form of shivering. When sufficiently warmed, the bees can fly.

Wind as well as temperature introduces an element of natural selection. The windy environment favors reduced or absent wings in grasshoppers and other insects. Of the ten grasshoppers species that breed on Colorado alpine tundra, only two have normal-sized wings.

The conspicuous presence of butterflies on the tundra is somewhat an enigma, considering the windy environment. Butterflies seem frail, yet those that grace midsummer blossoms can control their flight even in moderate wind. Their flight control is apparent to anyone who has ever tried to catch one in a net. Butterflies require relatively high body temperatures to fly and, like bumblebees, have evolved means to solve this problem in cool climates. The dark colors of the Phoebus parnassian and the Magdelena alpine butterflies help absorb the sun's radiation. Many species bask in the sun, orienting their wings like solar collectors, while others press their bodies against warm rocks. In fact, butterflies are able to maintain optimal daytime body temperatures almost as effectively as warm-blooded animals.

The distinctive long, clear notes of the white-crowned sparrow, drifting up from krummholz thickets or patches of willow shrubs, is often the first reminder that birds, too, frequent the tundra. Two of the most common summer residents, the American pipit and the horned lark, nest on the ground. The horned lark is also a familiar resident of prairie grasslands. The American pipit breeds strictly on the tundra, but announces its territory to other pipits in a way similar to prairie birds. Nesting in a land without trees from which to sing, the pipit flies skyward a hundred feet or so, then glides back to earth, singing all the way down.

A few species, including rosy finches and rock wrens, nest in rocky places. The brown-capped rosy finch is known to nest only in the high mountains of Colorado, northern New Mexico, and southern Wyoming, whereas the rock wren nests in outcrops from tundra to desert throughout the western United States. Ravens occasionally nest on precipitous cliff ledges above treeline. Other birds, such as prairie falcons, mountain bluebirds, and robins, are seen on the tundra but breed at lower elevations.

Only one bird species lives on the tundra year-round. The white-tailed ptarmigan, a small grouse with feathers covering its legs and feet, is superbly camouflaged for a tundra existence, altering the color of its plumage to match the season. In summer, ptarmigan are mottled brown, black, and white with white undersides, but in winter, their plumage is pure white, making them practically impossible to spot during any season. Hikers who have paused to rest on the tundra may notice a nearby "rock" starting to walk away. During winter, the only clue to a ptarmigan's presence on the snow may be its black eyes and beak.

Ptarmigan often sit motionless in the path of an advancing predator, or hiker, until practically underfoot. Then the ptarmigan explodes into flight, and that instant of surprise is usually enough to allow the bird's escape.

Masters of winter survival, ptarmigan weather storms by burying themselves in snowbanks, usually near willow patches. The snowbanks offer protection from the cold and wind and the willows provide their pre-

White-tailed ptarmigan, the only birds to live in the tundra year-round, change plumage with the seasons: summer plumage (right) and winter plumage (below).

ferred winter food: energy-rich willow buds. They eat so many buds that when spring arrives, they are fat and ready to breed, while other animals are in a weakened state. Ptarmigan nests are little more than shallow depressions on the tundra, lined with a few dry sedges and grasses. Fancy nests are of little use because fuzzy little ptarmigan chicks can scurry after their mother shortly after hatching.

Pika

Among tundra mammals, the pika is probably the most unusual. A member of the order that includes rabbits, pikas (also called conies or rock rabbits) do not act like rabbits and look more like small guinea pigs. They live in colonies among the rocks of talus slopes and felsenmeer and feed on nearby grassy patches. Always watchful, a pika colony erupts with sharp nasal squeaks whenever danger approaches.

As summer wanes, pikas start harvesting large amounts of foliage, which they store in hay piles among the rocks. They look comical, bustling about with a seeming sense of urgency, their mouths full of leaves and stems sticking out in all directions. Maybe that is why their warning cries may be muffled this time of year. Presumably, pikas are active all winter in their rocky havens, feeding on their stores of hay; but because their refuges are inaccessible, biologists know little about their wintertime habits.

Yellow-bellied marmot.

Other than deer or elk, one of the most conspicuous tundra residents is the yellow-bellied marmot. These large rodents seem to lead the proverbial "life of Riley," eating plants or basking on a rock in the sun. Actually, they are simply conserving energy. During summer, marmots accumulate large fat reserves to carry them through hibernation, in contrast to pikas, who work hard to store food for the winter. Marmots often startle hikers with a loud, piercing whistle that matches their other name, "whistle-pig." Though strictly herbivores, marmots have been known to crawl under cars to gnaw battery cables, radiator hoses, or other rubber parts. Fortunately, these unexplained eating habits rarely occur in the park.

Other small mammals also inhabit the tundra, including deer mice, voles, chipmunks, woodrats, and shrews. Other than the chipmunk, which interrupts its hibernation sporadically to feed, most are active throughout the winter. With all these smaller mammals to prey on, weasels are year-round tundra residents. In winter, these small predators shed their brown summer coats for pure white pelage and a black-tipped tail.

*R*arely seen, northern pocket gophers leave lots of evidence of their presence. Mounds of earth that they excavate while burrowing are common in grasslands and meadows, from prairie to tundra. During the winter, tundra populations tunnel extensively under snowbanks along the ground surface. In the spring, melting snowbanks reveal their organized lifestyle. Many of the snow tunnels are filled with soil excavated from the gophers' subterranean burrows, forming long, sausage-shaped casts called "eskers." Some snow chambers contain soft leaves marking dens, while others are pantries, packed with roots, bulbs, and tubers. Fastidious animals, pocket gophers fill still other chambers with feces.

Their name derives from their fur-lined cheek pouches, in which they carry food. Their lips, too, are unusual and difficult to visualize. Pocket gophers' lips close behind their incisor teeth, allowing them to dig without getting their mouths full of dirt.

Pocket gophers can cause considerable change to a tundra plant community, overturning as much as four to eight tons of soil per acre where populations are high. Their burrows frequently funnel meltwater, occasionally eroding into gullies several feet deep. On the other hand, pocket gophers help mix organic materials into the soil, much as earthworms do in other ecosystems. Many plants colonize the soft, bare soil of gopher mounds, forming "gopher gardens." Even abandoned gopher tunnels are a valuable resource. Voles, mice, and other animals use them for shelter.

Generally, elk migrate to the tundra from lower elevations only in summer, when they take advantage of the food provided by the lush growth of tundra meadows. Visitors frequently see them along Trail Ridge, and people stopping at the Alpine Tundra Museum can almost always spot a few elk grazing the meadows of Willow Park or resting in the shade of nearby krummholz stands. Although most elk return to lower elevations in autumn, a small herd remains in Willow Park through winter.

Mountain sheep, or bighorn, range widely over the park. Hikers encounter them crossing the tundra and motorists frequently see them near Milner Pass and along the north side of Horseshoe Park. The bighorn is the symbol of Rocky Mountain National Park as well as the official mammal of Colorado. Such recognition is appropriate because these animals are most at home in the rugged terrain that characterizes the region.

A glimpse of a mature ram with its massive horns can be thrilling. Unlike the bony antlers of deer and elk, which are shed each winter, sheep horns continue to grow. Both sexes have horns. The ewes' are small upright spikes and the rams' are thick, heavy, and spiral as they grow, sometimes curling in a full circle on the oldest rams. To support such weight, rams have not only thick, bony skulls, but also large neck and shoulder muscles.

Most bighorn sheep spend the summer on the windswept ridges and rocky ledges of the tundra. Hooves with soft, rubbery pads and pincer-like toes enable these animals to move with ease, even jump from ledge to ledge in this precipitous terrain. And their dense fur provides protection against stiff tundra winds. Bighorn rarely compete with elk for forage because they prefer high, windswept ridges, whereas elk browse meadows near treeline. Although forage on ridges is often poor quality, bighorn can survive on it because they have developed proportionately larger digestive systems compared to the park's other large grazers.

Young marmots tussle near their rocky den.

Some sheep remain on the tundra year-round, but many migrate to winter range at lower elevations, such as Horseshoe Park. During summer, rams roam in small bands apart from the ewes and lambs. Come breeding season, from November to January, the herds of rams and ewes join. Whenever a ewe comes into estrus and is receptive to breeding, the dominant rams kick, bite, and butt heads to determine who will do the mating. Often, fighting males become so preoccupied with their battle, that another ram will mount the waiting ewe.

A visit to alpine tundra holds many lessons. Its climate is harsh and unforgiving, yet the plants and animals that thrive here have developed remarkable adaptations for survival. It is a fragile land—damaged turf may take decades, even centuries to heal itself. It is a place where weather can change quickly, with potentially dangerous consequences for the unprepared hiker.

Yet, this realm has its softer moments, too. Tiny tundra blossoms delight us with their delicate beauty. We find pleasure in watching the antics of young marmots at play or in the unexpected discovery of a pipit nest hidden among sedge and avens. And we drink in the fresh, clean air. For these reasons and others, it is a land that demands greater respect and protection. It is a land that crowns the exceptional diversity of life found at Rocky Mountain National Park.

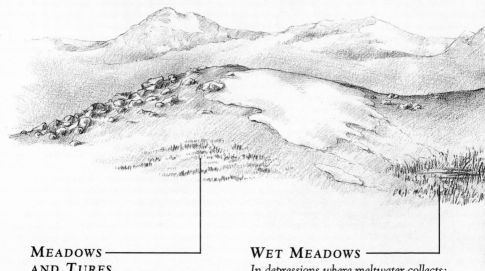

MEADOWS AND TURFS

Dry to moist slopes: turfs are in places that are windy and snowfree during winter and consist of dense carpets of grass-like plants; meadows occupy moister places and have a variety of wildflowers.

In turfs, look for the grass-like kobresia. In meadows, look for alpine avens, tufted hairgrass, alpine sage, and American bistort.

WET MEADOWS

In depressions where meltwater collects; often found downslope from melting snowbanks, or where shallow groundwater comes to the surface.

Look for marsh marigold, rose crown, elephantella, star gentian, and aquatic sedge.

ANIMALS AND BIRDS TO LOOK FOR:

Mammals:
Bighorn sheep
Elk
Ermine
Least chipmunk
Mule deer
Northern pocket gopher
Pika
Yellow-bellied marmot

Birds:
American pipit
Brown-capped rosy finch
Horned lark
White-crowned sparrow
White-tailed ptarmigan

Butterflies:
Chryxus arctic
High mountain blue
Magdelena alpine
Phoebus parnassian
Western white

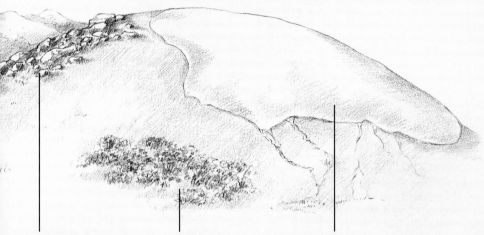

FELLFIELDS

Barren, rocky places exposed to the wind. At first glance, these areas appear to have no vegetation at all, but a closer look reveals plants that hug the ground or fill crevices between the rocks.

Look for cushion plants such as moss campion, alpine nailwort, alpine phlox, and alpine sandwort, along with mats of dwarf clover and mountain dryad.

SHRUB COMMUNITIES

In moist places where winter snow is just deep enough to cover and protect the shrubs, allowing them to grow taller than other tundra plants. Most shrubs in the park's alpine tundra are willow species.

Look for chiming bells and rosy paintbrush growing amongst the willows.

SNOWBANK COMMUNITIES

Underneath late-lying snowbanks, where the length of the growing season may be much shorter than in nearby areas because plant growth is delayed until the snow disappears.

Look for Pyrenian and black sedges, Drummond's rush, and the tiny clover-like plant sibbaldia. The whitish gray lichen Lepraria often covers the soil.

EPILOGUE

Rocky Mountain National Park is one of our country's most popular natural reserves. Several million visitors come each year to behold its wild and scenic treasures. This book was written so that they can better understand and appreciate some of the ecological relationships critical to the park. Such awareness becomes increasingly important as numerous environmental challenges to the park grow, because both the public and the National Park Service have a responsibility in determining the park's future.

The region has experienced many changes since prehistoric humans first hunted on Trail Ridge. Most large predators have been either eliminated or reduced to vanishingly small populations. Elk were extirpated, then re-introduced and now are so numerous that they threaten other resources in the park. Decades of fire suppression have subtly altered the ecology of the forests, and vegetative growth in some areas now has the potential to produce devastating forest fires. Park boundaries were established according to political expediency, but such boundaries have no meaning to wildlife populations or fire. Accelerated land development along park boundaries has resulted in a loss of wilderness quality. Proliferation of urban lights and visually intrusive roads, buildings, and other structures has psychologically "shrunk" the park for many people. If the wilderness value and ecological integrity of the park is decreased, the economic sustainability of the park's gateway communities also will decline: these factors are interrelated. Because of its close proximity to growing metropolitan centers along the Colorado Front Range, Rocky Mountain National Park struggles under an urban visitor load. Only an eighth the size of Yellowstone National Park, Rocky is attempting to accommodate the same number of visitors annually as Yellowstone; this places a tremendous burden on park resources. Entrance fees used to maintain park facilities have increased, and limitations on day use may soon become a reality to protect the park's ecosystems.

Morning mist over Dream lake following early autumn storm.

So what is the future of Rocky? The National Park Service has the duty to preserve and manage the park for future generations of people. But the park is not an island; it is surrounded by private and other public land beyond the jurisdiction of the Park Service. The success of management strategies in the park depends largely on how surrounding lands are maintained. The future of Rocky will rest on whether an effective and dedicated partnership between citizens, the National Park Service, and other government entities can be sustained. Understanding and involvement of the public is especially important. No one wants higher fees or to be restricted in their use of the park. Are there alternatives? What is the best way to preserve the park, yet make it available for the large numbers of people who wish to experience it? There are many issues, yet they are representative of what most of our national parks and monuments face.

Nevertheless, Rocky remains a magnificent jewel in our national park system. Its rugged landscape is as inspiring today as it must have been to the early explorers. Wildlife is abundant and accessible for people to watch and enjoy. The park contains some of the best examples of southern Rocky Mountain ecosystems to be seen anywhere, and it offers a multitude of opportunities for recreation and education. Wilderness solitude is available for those who wish to find it. Many citizens have become involved in trying to solve some of the park's management issues, and volunteer support in the park has reached record levels during the past few years. Rocky Mountain National Park is a remarkable place, and is symbolic of why we need to rededicate our efforts to preserve our national parks for generations to come.

BIBLIOGRAPHY

SUGGESTED READING

Many field identification guides and other reference books are available to enhance your enjoyment and understanding of the park's natural history. This list is not exhaustive, but includes publications that are particularly useful in the park. Most of these books are sold at the visitor centers in the park, or at local bookstores.

FIELD IDENTIFICATION GUIDES

Borror, D.J., and R.E. White. 1970. *A Field Guide to Insects of America North of Mexico*. Peterson Field Guide Series, Houghton Mifflin Co., Boston.

Burt, W.H., and R.P. Grossenheider. 1976. *A Field Guide to the Mammals*. Peterson Field Guide Series, Houghton Mifflin Co., Boston.

Carter, J.L. 1988. *Trees and Shrubs of Colorado*. Johnson Books, Boulder, Colorado.

Ferris, C.D. and F.M. Brown, eds. 1981. *Butterflies of the Rocky Mountain States*. University of Oklahoma Press, Norman.

Halfpenny, J. 1986. *A Field Guide to Mammal Tracking in North America*. Johnson Books, Boulder, Colorado.

Hammerson, G.A. 1982. *Amphibians and Reptiles in Colorado*. Colorado Division of Wildlife, Denver.

Lincoff, G. 1981. *The Audubon Society Field Guide to North American Mushrooms*. Alfred A. Knopf, New York.

Little, E.L. 1980. *The Audubon Society Field Guide to North American Trees: Western Region*. Alfred A. Knopf, New York.

Murie, O.J. 1974. *A Field Guide to Animal Tracks*. Peterson Field Guide Series. Houghton Mifflin Co., Boston.

Nelson, R.A. 1992. *Handbook of Rocky Mountain Plants*. 4th rev. ed. , Roger L. Williams. Roberts Rinehart Publishers, Niwot, Colorado.

Peterson, R.T. 1990. *A Field Guide to Western Birds*. 3rd ed. Peterson Field Guide Series, Houghton Mifflin Co., Boston.

Preston, R.J. Jr. 1975. *North American Trees*. M.I.T. Press, Cambridge, Massachusetts.

Pyle, R.M. 1981. *The Audubon Society Field Guide to North American Butterflies*. Alfred A. Knopf, New York.

Robbins, C.S., B. Bruun, and H.S. Zim. 1983. *Birds of North America*. Golden Press, New York.

Scott, S.L., ed. 1983. *Field Guide to the Birds of North America*. National Geographic Society.

Stebbins, R.C. 1966. *A Field Guide to Western Reptiles and Amphibians*. Peterson Field Guide Series, Houghton Mifflin Co., Boston.

Udvardy, M.D.F. 1977. *The Audubon Society Field Guide to North American Birds*. Western Region. Alfred A. Knopf, New York.

Ward, J.V., and B.C. Kondratieff. 1992. *An Illustrated Guide to the Mountain Stream Insects of Colorado*. University Press of Colorado, Niwot, Colorado.

Weber, W.A. 1990. *Colorado Flora: Eastern Slope*. Colorado Associated University Press, Boulder, Colorado.

Weber, W.A. 1987. *Colorado Flora: Western Slope*.University Press of Colorado, Niwot, Colorado.

Whitaker, J.O., Jr. 1980. *The Audubon Society Field Guide to North American Mammals*. Alfred A. Knopf, New York.

Willard, B.E., and M.T. Smithson. 1988. *Alpine Wildflowers of Rocky Mountain National Park*. Rocky Mountain Nature Association, Estes Park, Colorado.

OTHER PUBLICATIONS

Andrews, R., and R. Righter. 1992. *Colorado Birds: A reference to their Distribution and Habitat*. Denver Museum of Natural History, Denver.

Armstrong, D.M. 1987. *Rocky Mountain Mammals*. Colorado Associated University Press, Boulder, Colorado.

Benedict, A.D. 1991. *A Sierra Club Naturalists Guide: The Southern Rockies: The Rocky Mountain Regions of Southern Wyoming, Colorado, and Northern New Mexico*. Sierra Club Books, San Francisco.

Buchholz, C.W. 1983. *Rocky Mountain National Park: A History*. Colorado Associated University Press, Boulder, Colorado.

Cassells, E.S. 1983. *The Archaeology of Colorado*. Johnson Books, Boulder, Colorado.

Chronic, H. 1984. *Time, Rocks, and the Rockies: A Geologic Guide to Roads and Trails of Rocky Mountain National Park*. Mountain Press Publishing Co., Missoula, Montana.

Chronic, J., and H. Chronic. 1972. *Prairie Peak and Plateau: A Guide to the Geology of Colorado*. Colorado Geological Survey Bulletin 32, Colorado Geological Survey, Denver.

Colorado Native Plant Society. 1989. *Rare Plants of Colorado*. Colorado Native Plant Society, Estes Park, Colorado.

Cushman, R.C., S.R. Jones, and J. Knopf. 1993. *Boulder County Nature Almanac: What to See Where and When*. Pruett Publishing Company, Boulder, Colorado.

DeByle, N.V., and R.P. Winokur, eds. 1985. *Aspen: Ecology and Management in the Western United States*. U.S.D.A. Forest Service General Technical Report RM-119, Rocky Mountain Forest and Range Experiment Station, Fort Collins, Colorado.

Gregg, R.E. 1965. *The Ants of Colorado*. University of Colorado Press, Boulder.

Halfpenny, J.C., and R.D. Ozanne. 1989. *Winter: An Ecological Handbook*. Johnson Books, Boulder, Colorado.

Hansen, W.R., J. Chronic, and J. Matelock. 1978. *Climatography of the Front Range Urban Corridor and Vicinity, Colorado*. Geological Survey Professional Paper 1019. United States Government Printing Office, Washington.

Holt, H.R. and J.A. Lane. 1988. *A Birder's Guide to Colorado*. ABC Sales, Denver.

Keen, R.A. 1987. *Skywatch: the Western Weather Guide*. Fulcrum Publishing, Golden, Colorado.

Mutel, C.F., and J.C. Emerick. 1992. *From Grassland to Glacier: the Natural History of Colorado and the Surrounding Region*. Johnson Books, Boulder, Colorado.

Richmond, G.M. 1974. *Raising the Roof of the Rockies*. Rocky Mountain Nature Association, Inc., Estes Park, Colorado.

Siemer, E.G. 1977. *Colorado Climate*. Colorado Experiment Station, Colorado State University, Fort Collins.

Smithson, M.T. 1986. *Rocky Mountain: the Story Behind the Scenery*. K.C. Publications, Inc., Las Vegas, Nevada.

Willard, B.E., and S.Q. Foster. 1990. *A Roadside Guide to Rocky Mountain National Park*. Johnson Books, Boulder, Colorado.

Windell, J.T., B.E. Willard, D. J. Cooper, S.Q. Foster, C.F. Knud-Hansen, L.P. Rink, and G.N. Kiladis.1986. *An Ecological Characterization of Rocky Mountain Montane and Subalpine Wetlands*. U.S. Fish and Wildlife Service, Biological Report 86(11).

Zwinger, A.H . 1981. *Beyond the Aspen Grove*. Harper and Row, New York.

Zwinger, A.H., and B. E. Willard. 1989. *Land Above the Trees. A Guide to American Alpine Tundra*. University of Arizona Press, Tucson.

ACKNOWLEDGMENTS

The author is grateful to numerous people who contributed in many different ways to this book. At the very top of the list is my wonderful, loving family, for without their support, the book never would have been finished. Enormous credit goes to many professionals in the National Park Service. Glen Kaye gave initial impetus to the project while he was Chief Naturalist at Rocky, and the invaluable guidance and commitment of his successor, Jim Mack, carried the project to its end. Several Park Naturalists carefully reviewed the manuscript; the suggestions of Jeff Maugans and Rick Frederick were especially helpful. Ronald E. Thomas, Natural Resource Specialist at Rocky, generously gave his time and expertise with the Park's Geographical Information System in providing customized data files so that I could complete the maps. I am indebted to Curt Buchholtz, Director of the Rocky Mountain Nature Association, for his patience and support, and to Nancy Wilson, also of the Association, for her assistance. Jody Cardamon, a dear friend with the Aspen Center for Environmental Studies, carefully read and offered excellent comments on an early stage of the manuscript. David Armstrong, former Director of the Henderson Museum at the University of Colorado, reviewed the final manuscript. I thank all of these people for their contributions, however, I claim sole responsibility for any errors or inaccuracies.

Special thanks to the generous financial support provided by The Greenwich Workshop, Inc., Trumbull, CT and to artist Bev Doolittle and musician Paul Winter.

ABOUT THE AUTHOR

John C. Emerick is on the faculty of the Colorado School of Mines where he teaches ecology and other environmental courses. He has conducted summer field seminars on the natural history of Rocky Mountain National Park since 1980.

PHOTOGRAPHY

Perry Conway — Back Cover, 2b, 4b, 17b, 37, 52, 58, 69a, 73a, 76(inset), 78a, 79a, 85a, 91b, 94, 101b, 110(inset), 119, 129a, 133b, 137.

Kent & Donna Dannen — 1, 25, 32a, 39b, 40, 44, 48a, 61c, 79b, 80b, 85b, 86, 92, 95, 100b, 108, 109(inset), 117, 118b, 123, 127b.

John Emerick — 99b.

John Fielder — Front Cover

James Frank — 19a, 46, 66(inset), 72a, 122, 140.

Michael Lichter — 2a, 18.

Jim Osterberg — 71, 136.

RMNP — 11, 12, 15, 16b, 17a, 32b, 38, 87.

Wendy Shattil/Bob Rozinski — 16a, 31b, 41, 54a, 54b, 55, 59, 61a, 61b, 69b, 69c, 70, 72b, 73b, 78b, 80a, 81, 91a, 93, 99a, 100a, 101a, 102, 116, 118a, 124, 133a, 133c, 134, 135, 136, 137.

John Ward — ii, 3, 4a, 5, 6, 19b, 20, 24, 34, 39a, 42, 43, 48b, 49, 66, 76, 84, 90, 98, 103, 106, 109, 110, 111, 127a, 129b.

ILLUSTRATIONS

Bill Border — 8, 10.

Susan Strawn — 29, 45, 62, 64, 65, 74, 82, 88, 96, 104, 106, 112, 114, 120, 139.

MAPS & GRAPHS

John C. Emerick — 23, 27, 31(inset), 36, 50, 51

DESIGN & PRODUCTION

Ann E. Green, Green Design

INDEX

Page numbers in *italics* indicate illustrations. Scientific plant names follow W.A. Webber, 1990, Colorado Flora: Eastern Slope, University Press of Colorado. In recent years, he has reclassified many plants. Traditional names of affected genera are shown in parentheses.